Teaching Tumbling

Phillip Ward, PhD
University of Nebraska-Lincoln

Human Kinetics

Library of Congress Cataloging-in-Publication Data

Ward, Phillip, 1957-
    Teaching tumbling / Phillip Ward.
       p.   cm.
   ISBN 0-87322-497-3
   1. Tumbling--Study and teaching.   I. Title.
  GV545.W37   1997
  796.4'7--dc20   96-21955
                                                           CIP

ISBN: 0-87322-497-3

Acquisitions Editor: Scott Wikgren; **Developmental Editor:** Kristine Enderle; **Assistant Editors:** Julie Marx and Sandra Merz Bott; **Editorial Assistant:** Coree Schutter; **Copyeditor:** Denelle Eknes; **Proofreader:** Erin Cler; **Graphic Artist:** Kathy Boudreau-Fuoss; **Graphic Designer:** Stuart Cartwright; **Cover Designer:** Jack Davis; **Photographers (cover):** Wilmer Zehr and Boyd La Foon; **Illustrator:** Mary Yemma Long; **Printer:** Versa Press

Human Kinetics books are available at special discounts for bulk purchase. Special editions or book excerpts can also be created to specification. For details, contact the Special Sales Manager at Human Kinetics.

Printed in the United States of America   10 9 8 7 6 5 4 3 2 1

Human Kinetics
Web site: http://www.humankinetics.com/

United States: Human Kinetics, P.O. Box 5076, Champaign, IL 61825-5076
1-800-747-4457
e-mail: humank@hkusa.com

Canada: Human Kinetics, Box 24040, Windsor, ON N8Y 4Y9
1-800-465-7301 (in Canada only)
e-mail: humank@hkcanada.com

Europe: Human Kinetics, P.O. Box IW14, Leeds LS16 6TR, United Kingdom
(44) 1132 781708
e-mail: humank@hkeurope.com

Australia: Human Kinetics, 57A Price Avenue, Lower Mitcham, South Australia 5062
(08) 277 1555
e-mail: humank@hkaustralia.com

New Zealand: Human Kinetics, P.O. Box 105-231, Auckland 1
(09) 523 3462
e-mail: humank@hknewz.com

CONTENTS

As a gymnast, coach, teacher, and more recently university professor, I have participated in gymnastics over 25 years. Much of that time I have taught others how to teach gymnastics. Initially I directed that instruction toward coaches. However, during the past 10 years I have spent increasingly more time teaching teachers how to teach introductory gymnastics in schools and in school-like settings, such as clubs and youth programs. Beginning gymnastics instructors, whether they are teachers or coaches, face similar concerns, including: What do I teach? How do I teach it? Can I teach the skills safely? How do I know if the students have learned the skill? The goal of this book is to provide the answers to those questions systematically by creating options for the instructor to use. You can tailor the content of this book to your specific context.

The jump-off point for most gymnastics instruction is tumbling, which is commonly taught first because it requires little equipment and provides a foundation for more complex activities occurring with and on apparatus. I designed *Teaching Children Tumbling* as an introductory tumbling resource book for beginning instructors. It fills an important need for beginning instructors by providing a systematic curriculum with sequenced lesson plans, which most "how to" books do not provide. It is also a practical, usable reference for those who know something about gymnastics and want to further their knowledge. This book contains a set of skills and drills organized around skill themes designed to make teaching tumbling as efficient and effective as possible. You will find that the content of *Teaching Children Tumbling* is user friendly and will allow you

- to introduce children to gymnastics safely and correctly,

- to acquaint children with strength and flexibility skills that are important for wellness and health,

- to enhance the motor development of children, and

- to include a tumbling curriculum in your physical education classes.

In particular you will find the book filled with unique features including

- skills and drills accompanied by over 100 illustrations, with critical elements, cues and prompts to assist you in your instruction,

- 42 lesson plans sequenced to use with kindergartners to students in grades 5 and 6,

- several assessment options,

- a host of warm-up ideas,

- sets of task cards that you can copy and laminate for your students,

- a skill finder you can use to quickly and easily locate skills described in the book,

- a scope and sequence chart to help you see the "big picture" of structuring the content, and

- a resources and materials list.

Many school and community programs offer limited time and gymnastics equipment, and instructors have varying degrees of experience teaching gymnastics. I have designed *Teaching Children Tumbling* with these conditions in mind. The content is *teachable* by novice gymnastics instructors and *achievable* by students.

The book is organized into four sections. Chapter 1 has two parts: The first describes the recommended skill themes and instructional practices and the second part discusses movement principles for tumbling themes and skills. Chapter 2 includes an overview of the themes and skills in the book and provides a skill-by-skill description, including a diagram, list of critical elements, cues for instruction, and locations of additional drills to aid in the instruction. Chapter 3 presents a curriculum that organizes the themes and skills presented in chapter 2, covering six levels, each with seven lesson plans. Instructors can develop their own curriculums or use and modify the ones I present. The lesson plans in this section include objectives, equipment, and suggestions on how to present the content. Appendixes A through C include reproducible material, such as task cards for warm-up, counterbalances, partner balances, and a skills checklist that you can use to assess student progress. Additionally, there is a list of other recommended introductory tumbling and gymnastics texts and materials and an achievement certificate. I believe you will find *Teaching Children Tumbling* full of instructional suggestions and tumbling skills that will allow you to teach more successful classes.

ACKNOWLEDGMENTS

This book was originally developed from four introductory gymnastics manuals that I wrote for coaches in Australia during the 1980s. At that time, I was fortunate to work with two fine instructors: Trevor and Peter Dowdell. Both of these individuals played a significant role in my gymnastics education. Special thanks are due to Shannon Smith, who helped proof the text. Finally, I am grateful to my students, from preschoolers to international competitors, who taught me what works and what doesn't.

—Thank you.

Key

Skill Type

B = Balances
R = Rotations
S = Supports
S & L = Springing and Landing

Skill Finder

Number	Name	Page	Unit-Lesson	Type
36	Back rocker	21	1-4	R
37	Back rocker to stand	21	1-4	R
41	Back rocker with hand touch	23	2-4	R
47	Backward roll down incline to stand	26	4-3	R
49	Backward roll down incline to straddle stand	26	5-5	R
44	Backward roll down incline to tuck	24	3-3	R
48	Backward roll on mat to stand	26	4-5	R
51	Backward roll on mat to straddle stand	27	6-4	R
78	Bent-knee hop	40	1-6	S & L
9	Bent-knee stand	9	1-6	B
61	Cartwheel along a curved line	31	5-5	R
62	Cartwheel down an incline	32	6-3	R
63	Cartwheel on mat to stand	32	6-4	R
59	Cartwheel over an inclined rope	30	3-4	R
58	Cartwheel weight transfer along bench	30	3-2	R
18	Counterbalances	11	3-5	B
75	Couple jumping	39	1-6	S & L
81	Crab walk	41	2-5	S & L
42	Forward roll down incline to stand	23	3-2	R
40	Forward roll down incline to tuck	22	2-4	R
45	Forward roll from three different positions	25	5-3	R
39	Forward roll on mat to sit	22	2-2	R
43	Forward roll on mat to stand	24	3-4	R
46	Forward roll to three different positions	25	5-4	R
80	Frog jump (feet apart)	41	2-5	S & L
79	Frog jump (feet together)	41	2-5	S & L
84	Frog jump uphill (feet apart)	42	5-2	S & L
85	Frog jump uphill (feet together)	43	5-2	S & L
38	From stand to back rocker	21	1-4	R
21	Front support	13	1-3	S
33	Front support change to rear support	18	3-3	S
30	Front support to straddle stand	17	2-2	S

Number	Name	Page	Unit-Lesson	Type
65	Straight jump and land into hoop	35	1-1	S & L
2	T-stand	7	1-1	B
11	Toe stand	9	1-6	B
19	Tripod balance	12	3-2	B
6	Tuck sit	8	1-1	B
28	Tuck to front support	16	2-2	S
72	Two-foot bunny jumps	38	1-1	S & L
10	Two-knee balance	9	1-6	B
23	Wall walk to handstand	14	4-3	B
50	Wheelbarrow forward roll	27	6-4	R
34	Wheelbarrow walk	18	5-2	S

CHAPTER 1

Welcome to Tumbling

Tumbling skills serve as physical and conceptual prerequisites for more advanced gymnastics skills. Conveniently for novice instructors or beginning level coaches, we can categorize fundamental tumbling skills into three groups: balances and supports, rotations, and springing and landing. Each skill within a group is related to another by common movements and problem-solving themes. For example, the tripod, headstand, and handstand are types of balances. Performing these skills requires mastery of hand support and proper placement of the center of gravity. Because these skills share common solutions, it is both practical and efficient to group them together for instruction.

Before incorporating tumbling skills into your lesson plans or developing a tumbling curriculum, you should plan for effective lesson management. This involves reviewing effective teaching principles, assessment techniques, safety issues, and equipment needs.

TEACHING EFFECTIVELY

The teaching practices suggested in this book are based on thoroughly tested methods derived from research on teaching effectiveness. Key teaching practices include the following:

• *Maximize the available time for practice.* In each lesson we start with a certain amount of time. You can spend time during lessons on content-related activity, such as handstands, or noncontent-related activity, such as lining up or waiting for a turn. To make the most of your lesson, you must maximize the amount of practice time. To make sure this goal is met you should

- maintain control of the class,
- develop effective and time-saving management strategies (e.g., see following routines), and
- plan to spend most of the lesson on student practice.

• *Use class routines to save time.* Routines are managerial and instructional events that are a regular part of daily lessons. For example, commonly used managerial routines include using the same techniques for getting the students' attention (e.g., clapping or using a whistle), arranging students into different formations, setting up mats or distributing equipment, and taking class attendance. Instructional routines are often used during warm-up, equipment distribution, and lesson closure.

• *Use circuits to maintain newly acquired skills.* A circuit is a series or sequence of "task stations" where students move from one station to another. You can direct students to move from station to station after they complete the task at each station, or you can give them a time period (e.g., one minute) to complete the task before they move on. The direction to move on may be an instructor command, or it may be prompted by a prerecorded music tape in which music recorded for 10-second segments, indicating a change of activity, is followed by silence for 45 seconds, indicating the practice time. With this arrangement the instructor is free to supervise student progress while the music tape controls the pace of the lesson. I have used circuits extensively in the lesson plans in this book. Each circuit provides an opportunity for skill development, to review previously taught skills, and to assess student progress and achievement of the lesson objectives.

• *Assess what you teach.* Assessment is necessary to determine each student's progress but also to indicate if further instruction is necessary. When instructors observe students performing tumbling skills, their attention should focus on whether the student has completed the skill successfully. If the student is not successful, the instructor should assist the student in correcting his or her performance. If the student successfully performed the skill the instructor should praise the student. In either case, the assessment becomes a "component of the instruction."

• *Focus on skills refinement and mastery.* Researchers observing lessons in physical education have reported that instructors often do not use skill refinement (such as improving the technical performance of a student performing a cartwheel). Too often students progress through a sequence of skills without mastering them. A focus of instruction should be to refine student performance with the goal of producing *skillful, confident,* and *knowledgeable* performers. Using the skills checklist (appendix B) will assist instructors and students in meeting this goal. Allow students substantial practice time for refining and mastering skills.

• *Keep instruction and feedback brief, specific, and frequent.* Students need to know what the task is, how and where to do the task, and what the criteria are for successful performance. When you use feedback, you should assess its effect. For example, a student is performing a forward roll and the instructor asks her to place her hands near her feet as she begins the roll. However, the student doesn't place her hands close enough to her feet. To emphasize the instructions, the instructor draws a chalk mark on the floor and asks the student to place both her hands on the line. In short, instructor feedback and instruction must be judged by its effect on student performance.

Appendix D includes a short bibliography for those who would like to read further about effective teaching practices.

ASSESSMENT TECHNIQUES

Each skill in chapter 2 is accompanied by a description of its critical elements. These critical elements are also listed in the skills checklist in appendix B. Assessment not only helps determine what to teach by judging the current abilities of students, it also determines day-by-day goals for instructors. One way to implement assessment is to include a circuit in each lesson to review the skills in the previous lessons. The instructor can select one or two skills to assess as the students complete the circuit. At each station you could post critical elements for students as quick reminders and review.

A second way to assess student performance is to observe a sequence of skills performed in a routine. In addition to the assessment of critical elements, you might assess students on their form (how neat they were during performance, toes pointed, arms stretched, etc.) and on their construction of the routine (e.g., if they included the required number or type of skills). You can incorporate routines into different formats, including gymnastics concerts and student performances relative to an expectation or criterion. If you use this type of assessment, you must give students sufficient time to practice their routines.

SAFETY ISSUES

Gymnastics is an umbrella term that covers many activities, such as tumbling, apparatus gymnastics, rhythmic gymnastics, balancing, and trampoline. Some activities in gymnastics involve more risk than others. Many activities have evolved into sports in their own right, with specialist instructors to ensure effective instruction. Acrosport and trampoline are two examples. The content in this book avoids trampolines, acrosport, and aerial skills and focuses instead on achievable, safe, and fundamental tumbling skills. The skills and drills in this book are designed to help students experience maximum success, thereby creating a comfortable and secure learning environment. There are some suggestions for instructor or peer assistance, for example, when the need arises with students with disabilities or when a child has previously had a bad experience with a particular skill. There is not a requirement for constant instructor physical guidance for most students in the class.

You should observe the following safety guidelines when teaching tumbling skills:

- Provide plenty of room for students to perform the tumbling skills—away from walls, other students, and equipment.

- Insist that students behave appropriately—no running, teasing, or other inappropriate behavior.

- All tumbling skills should be performed on floor mats or panel mats arranged to avoid sliding.

- If you are using spotting techniques, teach students how to spot and give them time to practice.

- Students should dress appropriately for tumbling in shorts, T-shirt, leotards, or similar attire. Students should not wear jewelry, including watches or earrings.

- Before moving to more challenging skills, be sure that students have mastered the previous skills. Individual instruction may be necessary for students who are progressing slowly.

FORM

When tumbling instructors talk about "form" they are referring to body shapes that help create an aesthetic movement. The most common shape includes straight arms and legs, pointed toes, straight back and trunk (though often a curved or hollow shape is used), and slightly stretched neck. These shapes help in the presentation of the skill, and you should teach your students to perform skills with good form. A good rule to follow in tumbling is that most skills will start and finish in the "T-shape." When students are performing individual skills or a sequence of skills, such as a tumbling routine, the instructor can provide control and order by encouraging students to start and finish in a specific shape. Being in control is an important safety consideration in tumbling.

EQUIPMENT

The skills described in this book require equipment found in most elementary schools. In addition to floor mats or panel mats, inclines made from foam wedges or springboards are commonly used equipment. Please note that the size of your class and the lesson organization will determine the amount of equipment you need (e.g., circuits allow you to use many skills and different equipment and don't require a mat for everyone in the class). Each lesson plan specifies the equipment needed.

You can make other resources, such as task cards, critical element checklists, and achievement certificates as needed. See appendixes A through C of this book for examples.

HOW TO USE THIS BOOK

Although you can teach many fundamental skills using divergent teaching methods, this book presents two methods of direct instruction. For instructors who would like to construct their own program, or who would like to add tumbling skills to an existing program, chapter 2, titled Tumbling Principles and Skills, is most suitable. This chapter provides a step-by-step description of basic tumbling skills that includes an illustration, a list of critical elements, and hints for instruction. If appropriate, additional drills are listed to aid instruction.

For instructors who have little experience with tumbling instruction, or who wish to use a sequenced program of tumbling instruction, the curriculum in chapter 3, titled Curriculum and Lesson Plans, will be their choice. The curriculum organizes the skills across six levels, each with seven lesson plans. Each lesson outlines a day's activities into four blocks: warm-up, assessment and review of skills, and introduction of new skills.

Additional material, like the skill finder, the scope and sequence chart, additional resources and materials list, assessment forms, and reproducible task cards provides you with resources for your instruction. Used separately or collectively, these resources provide you with options to determine, not only developmentally appropriate activities for students, but also freedom to tailor instruction specific to your instructional setting.

CHAPTER 2

Tumbling Principles and Skills

Most tumbling skills attempt to solve common problems, such as overcoming gravity and becoming airborne, remaining balanced and stable, and beginning or ending movements involving rotation. Tumbling skills share common solutions to these problems, which we can describe and analyze using a few basic skill categories. We may describe the problems students face in tumbling as acquiring and maintaining stability during the performance of static skills (e.g., the headstand), learning to begin and end rotation, learning to spring into the air, and learning to land when contacting the ground.

BALANCES AND SUPPORTS

Acquiring and maintaining stability is an important consideration in tumbling. In this book, I

have categorized skills involving stability into two groups: balances and supports. A body is balanced if its center of gravity lies within its base of support. The center of gravity of a body is the hypothetical point through which the force of gravity acts, regardless of body shape. However the location of the center of gravity does not remain constant, but changes as the body changes shape (see figure *a*). The following examples illustrate the relation of the center of gravity to the base of support. Notice how the center of gravity moves as the shape of the body changes.

Principles of Balances and Supports

The following principles influence a student's stability:

The smaller the base of support, the less stable the student. For example, if you ask a student standing on two feet to stand on one foot and then

only on her toes, she will find it increasingly difficult to maintain stability because she has reduced her base of support to the toes (see figure *b*).

The lower the center of gravity to the base of support, the more stable the student. For example a headstand performed with the legs tucked is more stable than a headstand with the legs straight and extended upward (see figure *c*).

Teaching Balances and Supports

Early in your instruction, hold up a pencil and a rubber band that has been cut once. Ask the students, "Which is firmer, the pencil or the band?" Point out that, though not all tumbling shapes are straight like a pencil, all require the body to be firm. Continue by telling your students that "There are some ways of knowing if your body is firm. First, you should squeeze your tummy and bottom tight; when you hold these two body parts firm, the trunk of the body should be straight and

should resist bending. Second, it's important that the shoulders and neck be aligned correctly. Most often your shoulders should be down (this means depressed, not elevated); the neck should be elongated (not too stretched, but not with your chin on your chest either). With the head up and eyes looking forward, not up, you have a good body shape for most gymnastics skills."

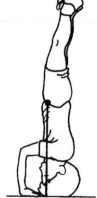
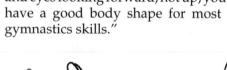

1. Standing tall

The student stands with body straight and stretched, looking forward, with shoulders down, neck elongated, and arms by her sides.

2. T-stand

The student stands with body straight and stretched, looking forward, with her shoulders down and neck elongated. She should lift her arms to her sides horizontally.

3. Landing shape

The student stands looking forward, with her knees bent slightly and the upper body leaning slightly forward. She should stretch her arms forward horizontally.

Teaching Tip

Have students land softly and quietly. This helps them absorb the force better.

Drill

Ask the students to jump and land in place, bending their legs but trying to make some noise. Then have them jump and land, bending their legs but doing so softly. Tell students that you don't want to hear them land; they need to be soft and quiet.

4. Stork stand

The student stands looking forward, with body straight and stretched, placing one foot on the inside of the other knee and hands on her hips. The student should hold this position three seconds.

Teaching Tip

Have students practice the stork stand on each leg.

5. Pike

The student sits on the mat looking forward, with trunk straight and stretched, shoulders down, and neck elongated. The legs are straight, toes pointed, and hands are on the mat beside the hips.

Teaching Tip

This is another important body shape for tumbling. Several skills start, pass through, or finish in this position. Many instructors, while demonstrating or instructing, have students sit in this position. It is also a great position for students to start a sequence from.

6. Tuck sit

The student sits on the mat balanced on the buttocks, with knees tucked up near chest and the toes resting on the floor. The student may place the arms either on the floor for support or wrap them around the knees. The student should hold this position for three seconds.

Drill

To make this skill easier, have the toes or feet contacting the floor; to make it more difficult, lift the feet off the floor. Also, wrapping the arms around the legs makes the position easy to hold. The more difficult position would be to rest the hands on the floor, and an even more difficult position would be to stretch the arms to the sides horizontally. As students try these positions, you might ask why some positions are harder than others to maintain balance.

7. Lying face down

The student lies face down on the mat, with his body stretched, arms overhead, legs stretched, and toes pointed. The student should hold this position for three seconds.

8. Lying face up

The student lies face up on the mat, with the body stretched, arms overhead, legs stretched, and toes pointed. The student should hold this position for three seconds.

9. Bent-knee stand

The student stands on the mat on one leg, with the other leg bent at the knee and raised to hip level. The student should lift his arms horizontally to the sides and hold this position for three seconds.

Teaching Tip
Have student practice the bent-knee stand on each leg.

10. Two-knee balance

The student kneels on the mat on both lower legs, with his arms lifted horizontally to the sides. The student should hold this position for three seconds.

11. Toe stand

The student stands on the mat on the balls of the toes, with her arms lifted horizontally to the sides. The student should hold this position for three seconds.

12. One-foot toe stand

The student stands on the mat on the balls of one foot, with her arms lifted horizontally to the sides. The student lifts the other leg off the floor, extended, and holds it slightly in front of the supporting leg. The student should hold this position for three seconds.

Teaching Tip
Have students practice the one-foot toe stand on each foot.

13. Straddle sit

The student sits on the mat, with the legs straddled (apart), with the arms straight and stretched overhead, shoulder-width apart. The student stretches the upper body upward at 90 degrees to the legs.

14. Knee scale

The student kneels on the mat with one leg, lifting the other leg straight, backward and upward. The student places his hands on the floor and looks forward.

Teaching Tip
Have students practice the knee scale on each knee.

15. Straddle stand

The student stands on the mat, with legs straight and straddled (apart sideways), and with the upper body bent at 90 degrees to lower body. The student stretches his arms horizontally and sideways and looks forward.

16. Shoulder-feet balance

The student lies on his back, with only his shoulders, feet, and arms touching the ground for support (i.e., arched). The student bends his legs.

Teaching Tip
During this skill the student should place no weight on the neck or the head. Instead the shoulders and arms should bear the weight.

17. Shoulder balance

The student lies on his back, pressing arms and hands down onto the floor, stretching his body straight above him, and pointing his toes upward. The student should place the hips over the shoulders and arms and look at the toes.

Teaching Tip

During this skill the student should place no weight on the neck or the head. Instead the shoulders and arms should bear the weight. The student can place the arms on the floor for support, or to make the skill easier, he can place the arms to support the back.

18. Counterbalances

The counterbalances are described in a series of task cards found in appendix A. The student should hold each balance for five seconds. To introduce counterbalances, group students into pairs. Explain the concept of a seesaw: "Two people of different heights and weights can balance at each end of the seesaw, and this is called a counterbalance. Note that even two friends of different sizes sitting at each end of the seesaw would be able to find a balance. The seesaw might not be level, it might instead be inclined, but a balance can be achieved. This exercise is about two partners finding a balance." Introduce each balance exercise separately and let students practice the counterbalance.

Drill

Counterbalance task cards are a great circuit activity to use for the whole class. To use the counterbalance task cards in a circuit, place the cards in a circle on the floor or on the wall, and give students (in pairs) 30 seconds at each station to demonstrate the counterbalance (you might need to have several pairs at each station). Rotate the students through all stations.

19. Tripod balance

The student kneels on the mat and places his hands and head in triangular formation. Next the student lifts one knee off the ground and places it on the elbow on the same side. The student repeats this for the other knee. Both feet are now off the ground. In this position there is a slight backward lean with the hands taking most of the weight (i.e., underbalanced). The student holds this position two seconds.

Teaching Tip

Introduce the tripod balance using the following two drills. When students can do both drills, introduce the whole skill by using a student to demonstrate. Identify the critical elements and demonstrate again with students looking for the critical elements. Allow at least five or six minutes of practice time for this skill. While students rest between attempts, have them watch their partners and provide feedback on the placement of the head and hands.

Drills

1. Demonstrate how to place the head and hands in a triangle by drawing a triangle on the floor using chalk. Have the students place their heads at the apex and their hands at each corner of the base.

2. The student should practice lifting one knee at a time (one foot always remains in contact with the floor) up onto the forearm while in the triangle position (hands and head).

20. Headstand

The student kneels on the mat and places his hands and head in triangular formation. The student lifts the legs one at a time upward, then joins them over the base of support (the triangle formed by the head and hands). The body is straight and stretched. In this position there is a slight backward lean with the hands taking most of the weight (i.e., underbalanced). The toes are pointed. The student should hold this position for two seconds.

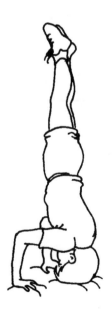

Drills

1. Demonstrate how to place the head and hands in a triangle by drawing a triangle on the floor using chalk. Have the students place their heads at the apex and their hands at each corner of the base.

2. Students should practice lifting one leg at a time (one leg always remains on the floor) up into the air while remaining in the triangle position (hands and head).

3. Students should practice lifting both legs in the tuck position off the floor a little at a time, increasing the distance slowly to a half headstand (a bent-leg headstand).

4. Do the exercise in pairs with one student standing and the other performing a headstand with one leg in the air and the other on the ground. The student who is standing holds the extended leg, while the student performing the headstand lifts the other leg up to join the

extended leg. One student is now performing the headstand and the other is holding both lower legs.

Teaching Tip

Ensure that all students have correctly performed the first three drills before attempting the headstand. The goal is for no one to roll or fall forward or onto his back. Always use students to spot each other (assist) when initially teaching this skill.

21. Front support

The student assumes a push-up position with straight arms, a straight and firm body (the back slightly curved upward), the legs straight and together, and the eyes looking forward.

22. Kick up to one-leg handstand

The student starts in a standing position, stretching arms forward horizontally. The student steps to lunge forward and places her hands on the floor shoulder-width apart. Keeping the back leg straight, the student kicks upward with it, and simultaneously pushes against the floor with the front leg, straightening it during the push. Finish in either near or momentary balance with both legs straight, one vertical (the first leg into the air) and the other horizontal or lower.

Teaching Tip

Introduce this skill by demonstrating it, emphasizing the importance of control. Use the following two rules to guide the instruction.

1. Progress from a small kick upward to increasingly larger kicks.

2. Don't have students attempt to kick past the handstand position (or they will fall over).

You might make a game of it by placing students in small teams and seeing if each team can perform the skill *without* falling over. Ensure that each student is well distanced from other students to avoid accidents. Additionally, try to have all the students face the same way. This will add some order and help create the self space for each student.

23. Wall walk to handstand

The student starts in a front support position with toes touching a wall. Then the student walks up the wall with each foot and walks toward the wall with his hands. Finish in a "near" handstand position, with hands about one foot away from the wall. Hold for two seconds, then reverse the technique (walk down the wall with the feet and away from the wall with the hands). Make sure that students walk (not drop) their feet down the wall.

Drill

Using chalk or tape, draw four horizontal lines, each one foot higher than the other (start at floor level). Each student should walk up the wall to the first line, then walk down the wall. Next, they should walk up to the second line, then down, and so on until they can walk up to but no farther than the fourth line. For some students the third line will be the highest they can walk without moving their hands closer than one foot from the wall.

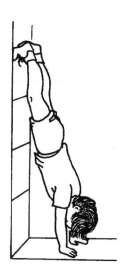

24. Rear support

This position is the reverse of the front support. The student starts by sitting on the floor, with his hands by his sides and legs stretched straight and together. Next, the student straightens his arms and lifts his bottom off the floor. The student straightens the hips so his body is straight from toes to shoulders. The eyes should look forward.

25. Side support

This position is the side version of the front support. The student sits on the floor with both hands placed on the same side. He should stretch his legs straight and together. Next the student turns sideways toward his hands and straightens his arms, while he lifts his bottom off the floor. In this position he should balance on the arm that is straight, using the other arm for support or extending it upward away from the floor. The student should straighten the hips and hold his body straight from toes to shoulders. The student should look sideways or down at the hands.

26. Game "Find the support"

This game requires students to run or skip until the teacher names a support; then the students quickly assume the support. The goal is to have every student quickly and correctly assume the position. The students can play several rounds of this game, providing at least five or six opportunities per support for practice.

Teaching Tip
This is a wonderful warm-up game and need not be limited to front, rear, and side supports.

27. Game "Under and over"

Divide the class into pairs, with each member of the pair numbered either one or two. The teacher calls out two commands: a support (front, rear, or side) and a direction (under or over). Students who are ones assume the position the teacher calls and their partners (twos) either crawl under them from the side or step over their legs (no jumping or leaping). Next, the ones and twos reverse roles. The goal is to see which set of partners can complete the task *without touching each other*. The students can play several rounds of this game, mixing the directions. Initially do not have students crawl under someone in side support, but introduce that combination later in the game.

28. Tuck to front support

The student assumes a tuck position with the hands shoulder-width apart. The student leans forward onto the hands and simultaneously jumps backward with the feet to finish in the front support position, with legs straight and together and arms straight.

29. Front support to tuck

Starting in the front support position, the student jumps the feet forward to a tuck position, with feet close to hands.

30. Front support to straddle stand

Starting in the front support position, the student jumps the feet forward to straddle stand. The student should hold the legs straight and apart and the arms horizontal and stretched to the sides. In the finished position, the body should bend 90 degrees at the hip.

31. Straddle stand to front support

Starting in the straddle stand position, the student leans forward onto his hands, while jumping backward with his feet to finish in the front support position, with legs straight and together and arms straight.

32. Game "Front support tag"

This is a typical tag game. Define the boundaries of the game, and nominate one to three students to tag the rest of the class (rotate students into and out of this role). When tagged a student assumes a front support position. To be freed a student who is free must crawl under a tagged student.

33. Front support change to rear support

Starting in the front support position, the student lifts one hand off the floor and turns over to rear support, replacing the hand onto the floor to maintain the support position.

34. Wheelbarrow walk

One student assumes a front support position with the legs apart. Another student (the partner) lifts the legs of the first student to hip level and begins to walk forward slowly, as the person in front support walks forward with her hands. The wheelbarrow walk should continue forward for one and one-half or two yards.

Teaching Tip

Introduce the wheelbarrow walk by stating, "The wheelbarrow walk is a seal walk without the need to drag your legs; instead your partner holds your legs" (see the seal walk, p. 42). Demonstrate the wheelbarrow walk using two students. Identify critical elements, and point out that the person holding the legs of the performer must be careful to go very slowly. Have the class watch again, and divide the class into pairs of students with similar weights. Specify the direction you want the students to wheelbarrow walk. Before starting practice, offer a reward (special activity, recognition, etc.) to any pair of students who can perform the wheelbarrow walk without either partner falling. The award provides additional motivation for students who might otherwise be careless. Do not encourage students to race each other as this can result in falls. If the person in the front support position cannot hold her legs straight, have the partner hold the legs above the knee to provide extra support.

35. Partner supports

Partner supports are described in a series of task cards in appendix A. Each card has a diagram of a partner support, and the cards are in order from simple to more difficult supports. Each card describes critical elements. The student should hold each balance for 5 to 10 seconds.

Teaching Tip

Introduce each partner support separately. Name it, state the critical elements listed on each task card, and let students practice the partner supports. Like counterbalances, partner supports are great circuit activities to use for the whole class. It is important to stress that partners should place support only *on shoulders* or *hips on the base student*, because these represent the strongest places in the body for weight bearing. Students should take care getting onto and off a partner. Get on by placing the hands on first, then each leg or foot; get off in reverse order, feet first, one at a time, then hands.

ROTATIONS

Rotation is the movement of the body around an axis. The axis can be a body part, such as an arm rotating about the shoulder, or the axis can be an object. For example, when we trip over an object, we rotate around the object (at least until we contact the ground). There are three generic axes around which our body rotates: (a) the lateral axis or side-to-side axis, (b) the anterior-posterior axis or middle axis, and (c) the longitudinal axis or head-to-toe. These axes are generic because they describe universal features of motion. The lateral axis describes rotation about an axis that passes through the body from left to right. This axis is commonly seen at the

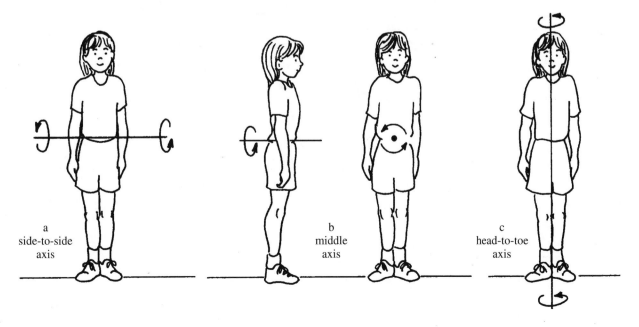

a
side-to-side
axis

b
middle
axis

c
head-to-toe
axis

ankles, the knees, and the hips during such movements as a forward roll or backward roll. The anterior-posterior axis describes rotation about an axis that passes through the body from front to back. This axis is commonly seen at the ankle, hip, and wrist during the cartwheel. The longitudinal axis describes rotation about an axis that passes through the body from top to bottom. This axis is commonly seen when the body performs a log roll or turn.

Principles of Rotations

When the center of gravity moves off center, away from the base of support, a body rotates. If a student is standing upright, to fall forward (a rotation) she must first lean forward. In leaning forward, the center of gravity moves off center and is no longer directly over the base of support. Changing body shape influences how fast a student rotates. A student can control the rate of rotation (how fast she spins) by bringing body parts closer together (spinning faster) or stretching body parts (spinning slower). In the illustrations below, if a beginner were trying to stand up out of the forward roll, he would have the most chance if he chose the tucked position to perform his roll rather than the extended position.

Teaching Rotations

It is helpful to introduce rotations about the lateral axis on an inclined surface. Foam wedges and spring boards covered with mats create inclined surfaces that make it easier for rotation to occur. When introducing rotations about the lateral axis, roll a large ball and a cube on the floor. Ask the students, "Why does the ball roll easily and the cube stop?" and "What can we do to make sure that we roll like a ball and not like a cube?" Curving the body during rotations about the lateral axis is an important concept. When discussing rotations about the longitudinal axis, go back to the cut rubber band and the pencil that you used when introducing balances and supports. Roll each on the floor and ask, "Why does the pencil roll easily and the rubber band stop?" Emphasize the importance of a firm body during rotations about the longitudinal axis. The principle skill that uses the anterior-posterior axis is the cartwheel. The key to introducing the cartwheel is to progress slowly through the initial drills.

36. Back rocker

The student sits on the ground in the tuck sit position. His back is rounded, and his chin is on or near the chest. Holding this shape, the student leans backward and rocks backward and forward on his back at least twice.

Teaching Tip
To make this skill easier, have students wrap their hands around their legs as they rock. To make this skill harder, the students can leave the hands stretched forward toward the knees.

37. Back rocker to stand

The student rocks backward and forward on her back. As she rocks forward, she uses her hands to push off the floor and simultaneously stands up, finishing in the T-stand.

Teaching Tip
To make this skill more difficult, ask students not to use their hands to push off the floor.

38. From stand to back rocker

The student starts standing tall, stretching the arms forward horizontally. The student then sits down slowly, using her hands for support on the floor. As the student sits, she assumes the tuck position and leans backward into a back rocker (rocking back and forth without stopping).

39. Forward roll on mat to sit

The student starts standing tall, stretching the arms forward horizontally. The student then tucks, placing hands close to feet but just in front of the shoulders, tucks the head toward the chest, leans forward, and pushes hard with the legs. This will start the roll. As the student rolls over he should maintain the tucked position. The student finishes this skill in a sitting position, with his legs straight on the floor.

Teaching Tip
Introduce the forward roll on mat to sit by reviewing the back rocker and by having each student perform the back rocker to sit on the floor four or five times. Be sure to emphasize hand placement and head tuck. Students should perform this task at least 10 times per class, with rest between each attempt. When you have only a few mats, alternate practices between two or three students sharing one mat.

40. Forward roll down incline to tuck

The student starts standing tall on top of the incline, stretching the arms forward horizontally. The student then tucks, placing hands close to feet but just in front of the shoulders, tucks the head toward the chest, leans forward, and pushes hard with the legs. This will start the roll. The student rolls forward in a straight line, finishing in a tuck position with hands on the floor in front of her feet.

Teaching Tip
If possible, it's a good idea to introduce incline skills within an existing circuit, because you may have only one or two inclines.

41. Back rocker with hand touch

The student sits on the ground in the tuck sit position. His back is rounded, chin is on or near the chest, and hands are by the ears, palms facing upward and backward. Make sure that the student's elbows point forward and not sideways. Holding this shape, the student leans backward and rocks backward and forward on his back at least twice, with his hands touching the ground behind his head each time.

Teaching Tip

For younger students, have them imagine that their hands are elephant ears and need to stay on their ears during this skill.

42. Forward roll down incline to stand

The student starts standing tall on top of the incline, stretching the arms forward horizontally. The student then tucks, placing hands close to feet, just in front of the shoulders. Next the student tucks his head toward his chest, leans forward, and pushes hard with the legs. This will start the roll. The student rolls forward in a straight line, pushing off the floor with the hands while standing up and finishing in a T-stand.

43. Forward roll on mat to stand

The student starts standing tall on the mat, stretching the arms forward horizontally. The student then tucks, placing hands close to feet but just in front of the shoulders, tucks the head toward the chest, leans forward, and pushes hard with the legs. This will start the roll. The student rolls forward in a straight line, pushing off the floor with the hands while standing up and finishing in a T-stand.

Teaching Tip
If you haven't already, it might be time to stop and improve the students' form as they perform the forward roll.

44. Backward roll down incline to tuck

The student starts in sitting position, knees close to chest (a tucked position) on top of the incline with her back to the incline. Her back is rounded, chin is on or near the chest, and hands are by the ears, palms facing upward and backward. Make sure that the student's elbows point forward and not sideways. Holding this shape, the student leans backward and rolls down the incline finishing in a tuck position.

Teaching Tip
If possible, it's a good idea to introduce incline skills within an existing circuit, because you may have only one or two inclines. Don't forget to emphasize arm push.

45. Forward roll from three different positions

The student begins the forward roll in one of the following positions: a straddle stand, knee scale, or stork stand. The student completes the forward roll as usual except for the starting position. The key points for the roll from these positions are to bend the legs and tuck the head toward the chest. The student should finish the forward roll in a T-stand.

Teaching Tip
Although three specific starting positions have been selected here, an alternative would be to have students create their own starting positions. One way to check for safety of the starting positions is to have students show you only the starting positions.

46. Forward roll to three different positions

The student begins the forward roll as usual. The student starts standing tall on the mat, stretching the arms forward horizontally. The student then tucks, placing hands close to feet but just in front of the shoulders, tucks the head toward the chest, leans forward, and pushes hard with the legs. This will start the roll. The student rolls forward in a straight line, pushing off the floor with the hands while standing up and finishing in a knee scale, a stork stand, or lying face up.

Teaching Tip
Although three specific finishing positions have been selected here, an alternative would be to have students create their own finishing positions.

47. Backward roll down incline to stand

The student starts in sitting position, knees close to chest (a tucked position) on top of the incline with her back to the incline. Her back is rounded, chin is on or near the chest. The student's hands should be by the ears, palms facing upward and backward. Make sure the student's elbows point forward and not sideways. Holding this shape, the student leans backward and rolls down the incline, finishing in a T-stand.

48. Backward roll on mat to stand

The student starts in a tuck position, knees close to chest, with her back to the mat. Her back is rounded, chin is on or near the chest. The student's hands should be by the ears, palms facing upward and backward. Make sure the student's elbows point forward and not sideways. Holding this shape, the student leans backward and rolls across the mat, pushing off the mat with her hands and finishing in a T-stand.

49. Backward roll down incline to straddle stand

The student starts in sitting position, knees close to chest (a tucked position) on top of the incline with his back to the incline. His back is rounded, chin is on or near the chest, and hands are by the ears, palms facing upward and backward. Make sure the student's elbows point forward and not sideways. Holding this shape, the student leans backward, straightening legs and pulling them apart. The student rolls down the incline, finishing in a straddle stand.

50. Wheelbarrow forward roll

One student assumes a front support position with the legs apart. Another student (the partner) lifts the legs of the first student to hip level. The performer (student in front support) leans forward, bends her arms, and tucks her head. This will start the roll. The performer's body rolls forward in a tuck position, and the partner holding the legs releases them. The performer finishes the roll in a T-stand.

Teaching Tip

An important safety test before pairs of students perform this skill is to make sure each student can perform the wheelbarrow walk. Students who can perform the walk have demonstrated that they can support their weight on their arms. Students who can hold the walkers' feet, without moving or pushing too fast to make them fall, can support their partners during this skill.

51. Backward roll on mat to straddle stand

The student starts in a tuck position with knees close to chest on the mat. Her back is rounded, chin is on or near the chest, and hands are by the ears, palms facing upward and backward. Make sure the student's elbows point forward and not sideways. Holding this shape, the student leans backward, straightening legs and pulling them apart. The student rolls over and uses her hands to push against the floor, finishing in a straddle stand.

52. Half log rolls

The student may start by lying either on her back or on her stomach, with her body stretched, legs straight and together, and arms stretched overhead and together, touching the mat. From this position the student rolls to the left or right, completing a 180-degree turn, keeping the body stiff.

Teaching Tip

Start with students lying on their backs and progress to lying on their stomachs, then from stomachs to backs, as well as rolling to the left and right. It is a good idea to arrange the class so they are all lying on their backs facing the same way, with approximately two or three feet between each student.

53. Full log rolls

The student may start by lying either on her back or on her stomach, with her body stretched, legs straight and together, and arms stretched overhead and together, touching the mat. From this position the student rolls to the left or right, completing a 360-degree turn and keeping the body stiff.

Teaching Tip

Begin with students practicing rolling from back to back, then from stomach to stomach. As with half log rolls, arrange the class so all students are facing and lying the same way. If possible, increase the distance between each student to three or four feet.

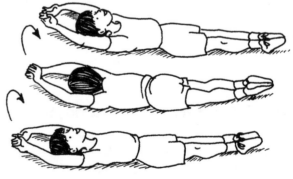

54. Puppy dog roll

The student starts kneeling on the ground on hands and knees. Holding this position, the student rolls to the left or right, making contact with the ground using shoulder, hip, and back and completing a 180-degree turn.

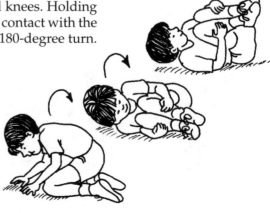

55. Partner log rolls

Two students lie face down, facing one another, arms overhead, and hands clasped. Both students have their bodies stretched, their legs straight and together. From this position the students roll together in the same direction for a complete 360-degree rotation. During the roll, the legs of each student remain straight and together, the arms remain straight, and hands remain joined with the partner's.

Teaching Tip
Introduce the partner log roll by reviewing the log roll, and have the class perform a few of these rolls. Divide the class into pairs of students. Next, demonstrate the partner log roll using one pair of students. Arrange the class so they are all rolling in the same direction (nominate a wall or direction). Make the task a minicompetition to see which pair can roll without breaking form (bending legs or arms or letting go of hands).

56. Sit and spin

The student starts by sitting on a mat, with bent legs and hands on the floor on either side of the hips. The student lifts her feet off the floor and uses her hands to spin the body around two or three times. During the spin, the student stays tightly tucked and wraps her hands around the knees. The student should always stay seated (don't spin on the back).

57. Jump, twist, and freeze

The student jumps into the air, with arms overhead and twists 180 degrees without falling, landing in the landing shape (see page 7).

58. Cartwheel weight transfer along bench

The student starts by standing with both feet on one side of a bench, facing along the bench. Leaning forward, the student places one hand on each side of the bench top. The goal is to transfer weight from one side of the bench to the other. To do this the student steps over the bench with the closer foot, followed by the other foot (a one-two action). The student repeats this action in reverse to step over the bench from the other side. The student should continue to go from one side to the other, stepping over the bench and moving forward for three or four attempts.

Teaching Tip
Allow one student at a time to do this drill. The bench ought to be low, not higher than 18 inches above the floor. If you have few benches, then use this drill as a station in a circuit.

59. Cartwheel over an inclined rope

The student starts by standing on one side of the rope, with his back to the wall. He places his hands on the floor on either side of the rope where it touches the floor. The goal is to transfer weight from one side of the rope to the other. To do this the student kicks up and over the rope with the closer foot, followed by the other foot (a one-two action). Though the legs may start bent, they should straighten as they kick off the floor. Continue to go from one side to the other, stepping over the rope for three or four attempts.

Teaching Tip
Emphasize hand placement and leg action. When you arrange this drill, affix the rope to the wall and the floor with tape so it will *easily* collapse if struck by a foot. (Do not use a solid pole because it will not collapse if a foot strikes it.) You can create several of these stations for practice.

60. Minicartwheel over a bench

The student stands in a lunge position perpendicular to the bench, holding arms forward horizontally (i.e., hands off the bench). Leaning forward, the student places one hand (use the hand on the same side of the body as the front foot), then the other hand, on each side of the bench top (a one-two action). Simultaneously the student kicks over the bench with the back foot, followed by the other foot (a one-two action). The student finishes standing on the other side of the bench in a T-stand. The student repeats this minicartwheel in reverse to step over the bench from the other side. The student should alternate performing minicartwheels and moving forward for three or four attempts.

Teaching Tip
This drill is similar to the cartwheel weight transfer along bench drill. Ensure that the student has performed the two previous skills correctly before introducing this skill. Like the cartwheel weight transfer along bench drill, allow only one person at a time to perform the skill. Emphasize hand placement and leg action.

61. Cartwheel along a curved line

The student starts by standing in a lunge position inside the curved line, facing toward and looking along the line, holding arms forward horizontally. Leaning forward, the student places one hand on the line in front of the foot (use the hand on the same side of the body as the front foot). Next, the student places the other hand in front of the first on the line. Kick the foot that is farther from the line into the air and forward, followed by the other foot (a one-two action). Finish standing farther along the line in a T-stand.

Teaching Tip
Draw a curved chalk line, or use tape to mark it out. Use as many lines as you have students in a group, if space permits. Make sure they are well spaced to avoid accidents. Students will typically favor one side or the other. Whichever side they favor should be the side closest to the line (e.g., if the left side is favored, the student should stand on the right side of the line with the left side of the body next to the line).

62. Cartwheel down an incline

The student stands facing forward, looking down the incline. The student stretches her arms overhead and parallel. Next, the student steps forward into lunge position and places one hand (the same side as the front foot) on the incline, followed by the other hand (a one-two action). This action will turn the body and begin the cartwheel. Simultaneously kick the farther foot into the air and forward, followed by the other foot (a one-two action). The student should finish standing beyond the incline in a T-stand, facing either sideways or forward toward the incline.

Teaching Tip

Use a small gradient on the incline. It helps to draw a chalk line down the middle of the incline and to tell students to place both their hands and their feet on the line.

63. Cartwheel on mat to stand

The student stands facing forward, looking down the mat. The student stretches his arms overhead and parallel. Next, the student steps forward into lunge position and places one hand (the same side as the front foot) on the mat, followed by the other hand (a one-two action). This action will turn the body and begin the cartwheel. Simultaneously kick the farther foot into the air and forward, followed by the other foot (a one-two action). The student should finish standing in a T-stand, facing sideways or forward.

Teaching Tip

It helps to draw a straight chalk line on the floor and to tell students to place both their hands and their feet on the line. Use as many lines as you have students in a group, if space permits. Make sure students are well spaced to avoid accidents. The placement should occur as hand-hand-foot-foot. Emphasize the start and the finish position.

SPRINGING AND LANDING

Springing involves projecting the body by forcefully straightening one or both legs or hands. Students can project their bodies by springing from (a) a leg, as in leaping or hopping, (b) both legs, as in jumping, or (c) using hands and legs, as in frog jump.

Principles of Springing and Landing

To correctly spring, the student needs a fast extension of legs or arms. Whatever limbs (legs, arms, or both) the student uses to initiate the spring, the action must move forcefully and rapidly.

Landings are important in terms of safety as well as control. Students landing with straight legs will demonstrate poor control of the landing and may injure themselves. Thus, when landing the legs should bend and absorb the force of the landing.

Make sure your students land with their feet apart. This is more stable than landing with feet together, because it increases your student's base of support. Stretching the arms sideways also increases stability upon landing.

Hips should always face the direction of the landing. Landing sideways is unsafe. Avoid sideways landings by teaching students to land with their hips facing the direction they are moving. It is important to note that it is unsafe to have the hip rotating at the same time the feet contact the floor. When this happens the potential for injury exists.

Teaching Springing and Landing

When teaching springing and landing, ask your students to picture how a rabbit hops or kangaroo jumps. Then explain that "when rabbits land, their feet are bent and their legs are slightly apart and they can spring into the next jump like this." Demonstrate a series of short hops, emphasizing bent-knee landings. Review the landing shape (statics) two or three times, then have students jump into the air and land in the landing shape. A perfect jump is one in which the student lands and is immediately balanced with no falls, stumbles, or steps.

64. Straight jump and land in self space

The student jumps upward, swinging arms forward and stopping the swing when the arms are overhead. As the legs leave the mat, they should straighten. Before landing the student should bend his knees and assume the landing shape. The landing should occur without stumbling.

65. Straight jump and land into hoop

Standing approximately six inches away from a hoop lying on the floor, the student jumps upward and forward, swinging her arms forward and stopping the swing when the arms are overhead. As the legs leave the mat, they should straighten. Before landing the student should bend her knees and assume the landing shape. The student should land in the hoop without stumbling.

Teaching Tip
Hoops should not require students to jump forward more than two or three feet. Use chalk or masking tape to outline a circle if you do not have hoops.

66. Star jump and land in self space

The student jumps upward, swinging arms forward and stopping the swing when the arms are overhead. As the legs leave the mat, they should straighten and move apart. Before landing the student should bring her legs together, bend her knees, and assume the landing shape. The landing should occur without stumbling.

Teaching Tip
This task requires students to jump forward and upward into the air, lifting their legs apart and landing in the landing shape. You could have this skill performed either in self space or into a hoop.

67. Jump over a hoop

Standing outside of a hoop on the floor, with arms by his sides, the student jumps upward, forward, and over the hoop, swinging his arms forward and upward. As the legs leave the mat, they should straighten. Before landing the student should bend his knees and assume the landing shape. The student should land on the other side of the hoop without stumbling.

Teaching Tip
Pay particular attention to the arm swing.

68. Jump backward into a hoop

Standing outside the hoop, with her back to the hoop lying on the floor, the student jumps upward and backward, swinging her arms forward and stopping the swing when the arms are overhead. As the legs leave the mat, they should straighten. Before landing the student should bend her knees and assume the landing shape. The student should land in the hoop without stumbling.

Drill
Begin with small jumps without looking backward. Have students gradually increase the distance. Introduce a chalk line as a barrier to jump over; then introduce the hoop. In the absence of hoops draw chalk circles.

69. Jump from low height with straight shape

Standing on the edge of a bench or raised platform, the student jumps upward, swinging arms forward and stopping the swing when the arms are overhead. As the legs leave the bench, they should straighten. Before landing the student should bend her knees and assume the landing shape. The landing should occur without stumbling.

70. Jump from low height with tuck shape

Standing on the edge of a bench or raised platform, the student jumps upward, swinging arms forward and stopping the swing when the arms are overhead. As the legs leave the bench they should bend upward into a tuck position momentarily, then straighten again. Before landing the student should bend her knees and assume the landing shape. The landing should occur without stumbling.

Teaching Tip
Students should tuck quickly, then stretch their legs for the landing.

Drill
Have students perform several tuck jumps on the floor first, before jumping from a height.

71. Jump from varied heights in star and tuck shapes

Standing on the edge of a bench or raised platform, the student jumps upward, swinging arms forward and stopping the swing when the arms are overhead. As the legs leave the bench, they should assume either a tuck or a star (legs apart) position momentarily, then straighten again. Before landing the student should bend his knees and assume the landing shape. The landing should occur without stumbling.

Teaching Tip

Have the class practice in self space on the floor without jumping from a height. Once students have mastered low heights, use a low stage or a higher bench to create different heights. Let students practice these skills by jumping off the raised platforms. Make sure you emphasize the landing shape (i.e., landing with legs bent and arms stretched out).

72. Two-foot bunny jumps

The student starts with legs slightly apart and bent, and performs continuous short and small jumps moving forward.

73. Kangaroo jumps

The student starts with legs slightly apart and bent, and performs continuous long and large jumps moving forward.

74. Mouse walk

The student begins on all fours on the floor. From this position the student walks on his hands and feet, "scurrying" across the mats.

75. Couple jumping

Two students stand facing each other holding hands. One student stands while the other jumps up and down continuously in the same place, extending his legs in the air and bending them upon landing. The students take turns repeating the activity.

76. Jack-in-the-box

The student starts in a tucked position, then jumps upward and off the floor, landing in the landing shape.

77. Jump and clap

The student jumps upward off the floor, and while in the air claps his hands together. Before landing the student should bend his knees and assume the landing shape. The landing should occur without stumbling.

Teaching Tip
This can be a fun game if you ask the students to clap their hands in different locations (e.g., above them, to the side, behind them), or you can challenge the students to clap their hands several times during one jump. To do so they must jump higher to stay in the air longer.

78. Bent-knee hop

The student stands with one leg bent at the knee, raised to hip level, and hops forward on the other leg.

Teaching Tip
Have students practice this on each leg.

79. Frog jump (feet together)

Starting in a tucked position, the student leans and reaches forward with his hands. While transferring weight from feet to hands, the student jumps his feet forward to tuck close to the hands.

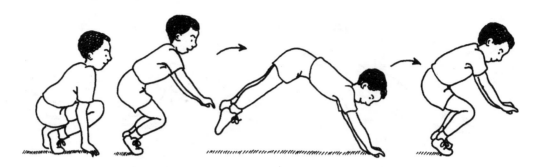

80. Frog jump (feet apart)

Starting in straddle stand with hands on the ground, the student leans and reaches forward with his hands. While transferring weight from feet to hands, the student jumps his feet forward to straddle stand outside the hands.

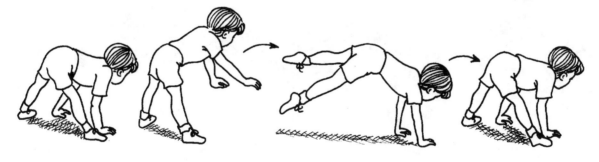

81. Crab walk

Starting face up, balancing on hands and feet with her bottom off the floor, the student walks forward or backward one step at a time (either hands or feet).

82. Seal walk

Starting in a front support position with the toes pointed, keeping her legs straight and together, the student walks forward by taking steps with the hands and dragging the feet.

83. Lame monkey walk

Starting in a lunge position with her hands on the ground, the student keeps her back leg straight and moves forward by hopping on bent leg, while pushing the floor behind with both hands.

84. Frog jump uphill (feet apart)

Starting in straddle stand with hands on a bench or raised platform, the student leans forward. While transferring weight from feet to hands, the student jumps his feet forward to straddle stand with his feet beside (outside) his hands.

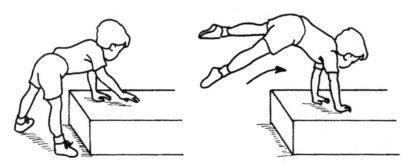

85. Frog jump uphill (feet together)

Starting in a tucked position, feet together and hands on a bench or raised platform, the student leans forward. While transferring weight from feet to hands, the student jumps his feet forward to tuck stand with his feet near or inside his hands.

86. Straddle over obstacle

Place the students in pairs. One student crouches with hands on the mat and the other stands two or three feet away from her crouched partner. The standing partner walks forward and places her hands on the crouched student's shoulders. The standing student jumps off the back feet, with hands remaining in contact with the shoulders, and straddles over crouched student, lifting her hands off the crouched student as she does so. The student should land in a T-stand in front of her crouched partner.

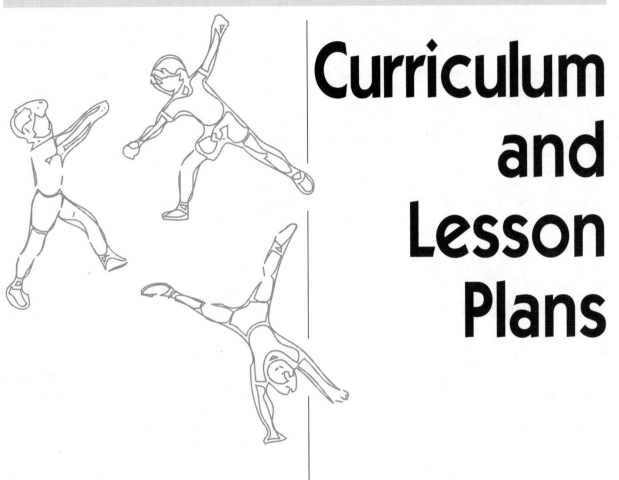

CHAPTER 3

Curriculum and Lesson Plans

In this chapter I have organized the tumbling skills presented in chapter 2 into lesson plans and sequenced them across six units of instruction. Each unit of the program corresponds broadly to grades K through five. For example, unit 1 is the beginning unit and is most suitable for students in kindergarten or grade one. However students in your class may or may not have the prerequisite skills in a particular unit. To avoid poor matches between the unit content and the students in your class, each unit has its own prerequisite check. The first lesson of each unit (except unit 1) provides an opportunity to evaluate the students' performance in class to determine if they have the necessary skills to master the content of that unit. Thus, teachers could use unit 2 or 3 with a grade four class if that class has not previously learned gymnastics or has not mastered the grade three material. Because the one-size-fits-all assumption of the lesson plan may

not hold true for your classes, please use the plans as a guide. The concept of developmentally appropriate instruction refers principally to matching the needs of the students to the appropriate content and instruction. Instructors should therefore adapt the plans as needed to their particular settings.

THE SCOPE AND SEQUENCE CHART

The scope of a unit refers to the selection of content you will teach in that unit. Similarly, the combined units represent the scope of this book. I have arranged the sequence of skills and activities within each lesson, throughout the unit, and across units. This feature allows teachers to pretest students at different units and to make individual and class decisions about the appropriateness of the unit skills. (Not all teachers will spend the same amount of time per lesson or per unit in this program.) During the planning phase of your instruction, use the scope and sequence chart to determine what content you will include. Because I have sequenced the book's content emphasizing skill development through refinement, removing a skill in unit 3 might remove a prerequisite skill needed in unit 4. The scope and sequence chart gives the teacher the overview so the decisions made in one unit do not unknowingly affect skills in other units. If you remove some content from one unit, make sure that future units include this content, or use the scope and sequence chart to plan your gymnastic curriculum.

THE LESSON PLAN

The content of this book, what to teach, in what order, and how to teach it, is based on more than 20 years of observations and instruction in gymnastics. Small and sequential teaching steps are presented to allow progress through extension and refinement of gymnastics skills. Each student in your class can achieve the content because I designed the methods to produce competency.

General Routine of Lessons

Each lesson is arranged into four blocks, warm-up, assessment and review, introduction of new skills, and closure. Warm-up typically includes routines either led by the teacher (units 1-3) or directed by task cards (units 4-6). The routines remain the same for the duration of the unit (though they change from unit to unit). Such routinization has several advantages, including efficient time use, an opportunity for student-directed activity, and a familiar start to lessons. The second block of the lesson plan is usually arranged as a circuit of activities that students have performed in previous lessons. This circuit adds skills that you taught in the previous lesson; thus the circuit is always changing, though its format remains the same. Because students know the skills and the circuit routine, teachers are free to provide individual feedback and assess progress during this phase of the lesson. The third block of the lesson plan introduces new

skills or refines and extends old skills. The introduction of new skills is either teacher led, whole group instruction, or included as part of an existing circuit of activities. Finally, closure provides teachers an opportunity to review the day's work, recognize specific performances, and motivate students for the next lesson by telling them what they will be doing. Because closure is specific to each class, none of the lesson plans specify what activities to include, but instructors will need three to five minutes provided for closure in the lesson organization. In general, lessons have been designed around 30 minutes of available time.

Lesson 1 of Every Unit

The teacher presents warm-up or warm-up tasks (using task cards) to students. Students learn the warm-up routines to use in each class and revise skills from the previous gymnastics unit. The exception is unit 1 in which the first lesson assumes no previous knowledge of gymnastics.

Lesson 8 of Every Unit

In each unit, seven lesson plans guide the instruction for the unit. However, these plans do not include a closing lesson. The teacher should create closing lessons to reflect the goals of the instruction for a particular class. The lesson might be used

- to provide further practice on skills not yet mastered,
- to catch up on students or skills not yet assessed,
- to provide a culminating activity for students to demonstrate skills they most enjoyed or performed well.

A Tumbling Concert

When you use the lesson as a culminating activity, the lesson may become a tumbling concert. You can present this in the same manner as a school concert. You need not limit such performances to the class, but might include other classes or visitors, such as parents, the principal, or staff. If you use this option, you will need to spend some time in preparation for the event. You can do this either by extending the unit one or two days to practice for the concert or by reducing the unit's content to spend the sixth and seventh lessons on concert practice.

I don't recommend treating the culminating activity as a competitive event. This is not because competition is inappropriate (though it is undesirable for the younger students), but rather it is inappropriate to place children in a competitive environment without preparation, both in readiness to perform the skills for a score and in readiness to perform in a competitive environment. It takes time to prepare students to compete, and it takes several systematically developed competitions to sensitize the student to the competitive experience. This is time that teachers frequently don't have available.

Scope and Sequence Chart for the Program Units 1 Through 6						
Unit	1	2	3	4	5	6
Balances	1. Standing tall 2. T-stand 3. Landing shape 4. Stork stand 5. Pike 6. Tuck sit 7. Lying face down 8. Lying face up 9. Game "Balance 1-2-3" 10. Bent-knee stand 11. Two-knee balance 12. Toe stand 13. One-foot toe stand	1. Straddle sit 2. Knee scale 3. Straddle stand 4. Shoulder-feet balance	1. Shoulder balance 2. Tripod balance 3. Counter-balances	1. Headstand 2. Wall walk to hand-stand	1. Headstand 2. Wall walk to hand-stand 3. Kick up to one-leg handstand	1. Headstand 2. Wall walk to hand-stand 3. Kick up to one-leg handstand
Supports	1. Front support 2. Rear support 3. Side support 4. Game "Find the support" 5. Game "Under and over"	1. Tuck to front support 2. Front support to tuck 3. Front support to straddle stand 4. Straddle stand to front support	1. Front support change to rear support 2. Game "Front support tag"		1. Wheel-barrow walk	1. Partner supports

Unit	1	2	3	4	5	6
Rotations	*Side-to-side* 1. Back rocker 2. Back rocker to stand 3. From stand to back rocker	1. Forward roll on mat to sit 2. Forward roll down incline to tuck 3. Back rocker with hand touch	1. Forward roll down incline to stand 2. Forward roll on mat to stand 3. Backward roll down incline to tuck	1. Forward roll on mat to stand 2. Backward roll down incline to stand 3. Backward roll on mat to stand	1. Forward roll from three different positions 2. Forward roll to three different positions 3. Backward roll on mat to stand 4. Backward roll down incline to straddle stand	1. Wheelbarrow forward roll 2. Backward roll on mat to straddle stand
	Middle		1. Cartwheel weight transfer along bench 2. Cartwheel over an inclined rope	1. Cartwheel over an inclined rope 2. Mini-cartwheel over a bench	1. Mini-cartwheel over a bench 2. Cartwheel along a curved line	1. Cartwheel along a curved line 2. Cartwheel down an incline 3. Cartwheel on mat to stand
	Head-to-toe 1. Half log rolls 2. Full log rolls 3. Puppy dog roll	1. Partner log rolls	1. Sit and spin 2. Jump, twist, and freeze			

Unit	1	2	3	4	5	6
Springing	1. Two-foot bunny jumps 2. Kangaroo jumps 3. Mouse walk 4. Couple jumping 5. Jack-in-the-box 6. Jump and clap 7. Bent-knee hop	1. Frog jump (feet together) 2. Frog jump (feet apart) 3. Crab walk	1. Seal walk 2. Lame monkey walk	1. Lame monkey walk 2. Frog jump (feet apart) 3. Frog jump (feet together)	1. Frog jump uphill (feet apart) 2. Frog jump uphill (feet together)	1. Straddle over obstacle
Landing	1. Straight jump and land in self space 2. Straight jump and land into hoop 3. Star jump and land in self space 4. Game "In the forest" 5. Game "Stop and go"	1. Jump over a hoop 2. Jump backward into a hoop	1. Jump from low height with straight shape	1. Jump from low height with tuck shape	1. Jump from varied heights in star and tuck shapes	

1-1

The following tasks should be accomplished in this lesson:

New Skills

Balances

Standing tall
T-stand
Landing shape
Stork stand
Pike
Tuck sit
Lying face down
Lying face up
Game "Balance 1-2-3"

Springing and Landing

Straight jump and land in self space
Straight jump and land into hoop
Star jump and land in self space
Two-foot bunny jumps
Kangaroo jumps
Mouse walk
Game "In the forest"

Equipment

Mats
Open area clear of obstacles

WARM-UP ACTIVITIES (3-5 MINUTES)

Game "Stop and go"

The teacher says to students, "I have a new game for us to play. It's called 'Stop and go.' I will tell you either to walk or to run. Then, when I say STOP I want you to stop moving, and when I say GO I want you to move the way I tell you to. Let's try it. I want you to walk quickly around inside this area. . . . Go. . . . Stop." Repeat with similar traveling tasks, such as running, hopping, and skipping.

NEW SKILLS (20-25 MINUTES)

Balances

1. Introduce a balance by naming it ("This is a T-stand."), demonstrating it (you or a student), identifying the critical elements ("Did you see how my arms were up like an airplane, and my body was straight?"), and demonstrating again, with students looking for the critical elements ("I'm going to demonstrate the T-stand again. Let's see if you can tell me if I am doing it correctly or not."). You might make a mistake or two (e.g., bent arms) in order to have students discriminate errors. Then let the students practice in self space.

2. Introduce all the balances using this method.

3. Next, play the game "Balance 1-2-3." The teacher says the name of the balance (e.g., T-stand), then "Balance 1-2-3" representing three seconds for students to hold the balance. Go through each balance several times using this game.

Springing and Landing

1. Gather the students and ask them, "How do kangaroos jump?" Select the child who most correctly explains the two-foot jump. Have that child demonstrate the skill with the class watching; then play the "Stop and go" game, with the class jumping as kangaroos. Repeat this procedure for two-foot bunny jumps and the mouse walk.

2. Play the game "In the forest." The teacher says to the students, "In the forest I see . . ." and names either kangaroos or mice. Students begin to imitate the animal named. Whenever the teacher begins to say, "In the forest" the students should stop and listen so they know what animal to move like.

3. Use the same technique you used with the balances to introduce the straight jump and land in self space, straight jump and land into hoop, and star jump and land in self space.

1-2

The following tasks should be accomplished in this lesson:

Review

Balances

Standing tall
T-stand
Landing shape
Stork stand
Pike
Tuck sit
Lying face down
Lying face up
Game "Balance 1-2-3"

Springing and Landing

Straight jump and land in self space
Straight jump and land into hoop
Star jump and land in self space
Two-foot bunny jumps
Kangaroo jumps
Mouse walk
Game "In the forest"

New Skills

Rotations

Half log rolls
Full log rolls
Puppy dog roll

Equipment

Mats
Open area clear of obstacles
Bat or a round pole for demonstrating rolling

WARM-UP ACTIVITIES (3 MINUTES)

Play the "Stop and go" game using different locomotions (see lesson 1).

REVIEW (12 MINUTES)

Balances

1. Review each of the balances by naming it and asking the class to demonstrate it. Review critical elements and correct errors. Repeat this procedure for each balance.

2. Play the game "Balance 1-2-3" (see lesson 1). Go through each balance at least three times using this game.

Springing and Landing

1. Gather the students and review each of the animal walks (two-foot bunny jumps, kangaroo jumps, and mouse walk) by naming it and asking the class to demonstrate it. Review critical elements and correct errors.

2. Play the game "In the forest" (see lesson 1). Allow at least three or four opportunities to practice each animal walk and approximately 15 to 20 seconds per opportunity.

3. Review the straight jump and land in self space, straight jump and land into hoop, and star jump and land in self space by naming them and asking the class to demonstrate them. Review critical elements and correct errors. Each child should practice each landing at least four or five times. Play a game to see who lands balanced.

NEW SKILLS (10 MINUTES)

Rotations

1. Introduce the concept of rolling by rolling a bat or stick across the floor. Ask students to try to maintain a stretched position like the stick when they log roll.

2. Using this concept, introduce the half log rolls. Name the skill and have a student demonstrate it. Identify the critical elements and ask students to watch another demonstration to look for them. Arrange the class so they are all facing the same way, lying on their backs with two to four feet between each student (use rows and columns for organization). Have the class roll in the same direction onto their stomachs, then back again onto their backs. Choose the other direction and repeat the exercise.

3. Next, tell the class that you are going to clap. When you clap they should roll in the opposite direction that they last rolled. First, they will roll onto their stomachs, then onto their backs. Repeat this several times.

4. Use this procedure to introduce the full log rolls. Using hand claps have the class complete one roll to the left, then one roll to the right, or multiple rolls (two or three) in one direction.

5. Use the same procedure to introduce the puppy dog roll.

1-3

The following tasks should be accomplished in this lesson:

Assess

Balances

Standing tall
T-stand
Landing shape
Stork stand
Pike
Tuck sit
Lying face down
Lying face up

Review

Rotations

Half log rolls
Full log rolls
Puppy dog roll

Springing and Landing

Straight jump and land in self space
Straight jump and land into hoop
Star jump and land in self space
Two-foot bunny jumps
Kangaroo jumps
Mouse walk

New Skills

Supports

Front support
Rear support
Side support
Game "Find the support"

Equipment

Mats
Open area clear of obstacles

WARM-UP ACTIVITIES (3-5 MINUTES)

Play the game "In the forest" to review animal walks. Students should know this game well by now.

ASSESS (5-7 MINUTES)

Balances

Using the skills checklist (see appendix B) and the game "Balance 1-2-3" assess the students in your class on their performance of each balance. An easy and efficient way to do this assessment is to choose a skill and two critical elements, and observe students as they perform the skill. *Look for errors.* Then have the class perform the skill again; this time look for other critical elements. If you are unsure of a performance, ask a student to perform it again or observe the student as the class performs the skill again. In this manner you can observe all the tasks in five to seven minutes.

REVIEW (7 MINUTES)

Rotations

Review the half log rolls. Have the class perform once or twice and review the critical elements. Then let the class practice it again. Use the same procedure (practice, review critical elements, and practice) to review the full log rolls and the puppy dog roll. Allow ample opportunities to roll in both directions, and start the half log rolls and full log rolls on the back as well as the stomach.

Springing and Landing

Review straight jump and land in self space, straight jump and land into hoop, and star jump and land in self space. Each child should practice each landing at least four or five times. Play the game to see who lands balanced.

NEW SKILLS (10 MINUTES)

Supports

1. Introduce the front support by demonstrating it. Identify critical elements, and ask students to look for them as the support is demonstrated again. Students should then practice in self space. Use this procedure (demonstrate, review critical elements, demonstrate, and practice) to introduce the rear and side supports.

2. Introduce the game "Find the support." Gather students and inform them that they are going to play a new game called "Find the support." This game is similar to "In the forest." Students may walk, run, or skip within a defined area (you could use cones to mark off the area). When you name a support, the students must quickly assume that support. The goal is to have every student quickly and correctly assume the position. Play the game several times, providing at least five or six opportunities per support for practice.

1-4

The following tasks should be accomplished in this lesson:

Assess

Springing and Landing

Two-foot bunny jumps
Kangaroo jumps
Mouse walk
Assess any remaining balances from the previous lesson (standing tall, T-stand, landing shape, stork stand, pike, tuck sit, lying face down, lying face up).

Review

Supports

Front support
Rear support
Side support

Rotations

Half log rolls
Full log rolls
Puppy dog roll

Springing and Landing

Straight jump and land in self space
Straight jump and land into hoop
Star jump and land in self space

New Skills

Rotations

Back rocker
Back rocker to stand
From stand to back rocker

Equipment

Mats
Open area clear of obstacles

WARM-UP ACTIVITIES (5 MINUTES)

Play the game "In the forest." During the game use the skills checklist to assess each student's performance on each of the springing and landing skills.

ASSESS (5 MINUTES)

Balances

Assess any students or balances that you did not assess previously, using skills checklist and the game "Balance 1-2-3."

REVIEW (9 MINUTES)

Supports

1. Review the front support, rear support, and side support by asking the class to demonstrate each skill. Restate the critical elements and correct any errors.

2. Next, play the game "Find the support." Play the game several times, providing at least five or six opportunities per support for practice.

Rotations

1. Review the half log rolls. Have the class perform once or twice and review the critical elements. Then let the class practice it again.

2. Use the same procedure (practice, review critical elements, and practice) to review the full log rolls and the puppy dog roll. Allow ample opportunities to roll in both directions, and start the half log rolls and full log rolls on the back as well as the stomach.

Springing and Landing

Practice straight jump and land in self space, straight jump and land into hoop, and star jump and land in self space at least four or five times as a game to see who lands balanced.

NEW SKILLS (10 MINUTES)

Rotations

1. Introduce the back rocker by demonstrating it, identifying critical elements, and demonstrating it again asking students to look for the critical elements. Then allow students to practice it in self space 6 to 10 times. Look for common errors, and bring the class together to review the common errors and critical elements. Allow time for more practice and correct individual errors.

2. Use the same procedure for the back rocker to stand and from stand to back rocker. Note that you will probably need to provide several opportunities for students to observe the critical elements correctly performed and more opportunity to practice than any of the past skills.

1-5

The following tasks should be accomplished in this lesson:

Assess

Rotations

Half log rolls
Full log rolls
Puppy dog roll

Springing and Landing

Straight jump and land in self space
Straight jump and land into hoop
Star jump and land in self space

Review

Rotations

Back rocker
Back rocker to stand
From stand to back rocker

Supports

Front support
Rear support
Side support

Springing and Landing

Two-foot bunny jumps
Kangaroo jumps
Mouse walk

Balances

Standing tall
T-stand
Landing shape
Stork stand
Pike
Tuck sit
Lying face down
Lying face up
Game "Balance 1-2-3"

New Skills

Supports

Game "Under and over"

Equipment

Mats
Open area clear of obstacles

WARM-UP ACTIVITIES (3-5 MINUTES)

Play the game "In the forest" and review the animal walks.

ASSESS (7 MINUTES)

Rotations

Assess the half log rolls, full log rolls, and puppy dog roll as the students perform each.

Springing and Landing

Play a game to see who lands balanced, and assess the straight jump and land in self space, straight jump and land into hoop, and star jump and land in self space.

REVIEW (7 MINUTES)

Rotations

1. Review the back rocker, asking the class to demonstrate it. Restate the critical elements; then allow students to practice it in self space. Look for common errors and correct them.

2. Using the same procedure, review the back rocker to stand and from stand to back rocker.

Provide at least 10 opportunities per task during this session.

Balances

Play the game "Balance 1-2-3" to review the balances.

NEW SKILLS (10 MINUTES)

Supports

1. Review the game "Find the support" two or three times.

2. Introduce a variation of "Find the support" called "Under and over." Divide the class into pairs, with each member of the pair numbered either one or two. The teacher calls out two commands: a support (front, rear, or side) and a direction (under or over). Students who are ones assume the position called by the teacher, and their partners (twos) either crawl under them from the side or step over their legs (no jumping or leaping). Next, the ones and twos reverse roles. The goal is to see which set of partners can *both* complete the task *without touching each other*. You can play several rounds of this game, mixing the directions. Initially do not have students crawl under someone in side support, but introduce that combination later in the game. Demonstrate using one or two pairs of students. Then divide the class into pairs. Have the class practice each combination once. Look for errors leaping or jumping over, or partners touching each other during the crawl. Make sure you have allowed enough space between students to avoid collisions.

1-6

The following tasks should be accomplished in this lesson:

Assess

Rotations

Back rocker
Back rocker to stand
From stand to back rocker

Review

Supports

Front support
Rear support
Side support

Springing and Landing

Two-foot bunny jumps
Kangaroo jumps
Mouse walk

Balances

Standing tall
T-stand
Landing shape
Stork stand
Pike
Tuck sit
Lying face down
Lying face up

Rotations

Half log rolls
Full log rolls
Puppy dog roll

New Skills

Balances

Bent-knee stand
Two-knee balance
Toe stand
One-foot toe stand

Springing and Landing

Couple jumping
Jack-in-the-box
Jump and clap
Bent-knee hop

Equipment

Mats
Open area clear of obstacles

WARM-UP ACTIVITIES (6 MINUTES)

Play the games "In the forest" and "Under and over."

ASSESS (6 MINUTES)

Rotations

Assess the back rocker, back rocker to stand, and from stand to back rocker. Provide at least two or three opportunities per task before assessing.

REVIEW (3 MINUTES)

Rotations

Practice the half log rolls, the full log rolls, and the puppy dog roll. Allow ample opportunities to roll in both directions, and start the half log rolls and full log rolls on the back as well as the stomach.

NEW SKILLS (13 MINUTES)

Balances

1. Play the game "Balance 1-2-3." Introduce bent-knee stand, two-knee balance, toe stand, and one-foot toe stand in the following way. Present each skill one at a time. Name it, demonstrate it (you or students), identify critical elements, and have class observe another demonstration. Then the whole class practices it. Correct errors, then introduce the next balance.

2. Next, play a new version of "Balance 1-2-3" using only the new skills. Allow lots of opportunities for practice, and correct errors.

Springing and Landing

Introduce the skills couple jumping, jack-in-the-box, jump and clap, and bent-knee hop the way you did the previous balances. Present each skill one at a time. Name the skill, demonstrate it, identify critical elements, and have class observe another demonstration. Then the whole class practices it. Correct errors, then introduce the next balance.

1-7

The following tasks should be accomplished in this lesson:

Assess

Balances

Bent-knee stand
Two-knee balance
Toe stand
One-foot toe stand

Springing and Landing

Couple jumping
Jack-in-the-box
Jump and clap
Bent-knee hop

Review

Supports

Front support
Rear support
Side support

Springing and Landing

Two-foot bunny jumps
Kangaroo jumps
Mouse walk

Rotations

Half log rolls
Full log rolls
Puppy dog roll
Back rocker
Back rocker to stand
From stand to back rocker

Equipment

Mats
Open area clear of obstacles

WARM-UP ACTIVITIES (5 MINUTES)

Review the springing and landing skills: two-foot bunny jumps, kangaroo jumps, and mouse walk using the game "In the forest."

ASSESS (11 MINUTES)

Balances

Assess the bent-knee stand, two-knee balance, toe stand, and one-foot toe stand during the game "Balance 1-2-3."

Springing and Landing

Assess couple jumping, jack-in-the-box, jump and clap, and bent-knee hop as the class performs each one.

REVIEW (8 MINUTES)

Supports

Review front, rear, and side supports during the game "Find the support."

Rotations

Review half log rolls, full log rolls, puppy dog roll, back rocker, back rocker to stand, and from stand to back rocker individually or in a circuit.

2-1

The following tasks should be accomplished in this lesson:

Review and Assess

Supports

Front support
Rear support
Side support
Game "Find the support"

Balances

Standing tall
T-stand
Landing shape
Pike
Tuck sit
Game "Balance 1-2-3"

Rotations

Back rocker
Back rocker to stand
From stand to back rocker
Full log rolls

Equipment

Mats
Open area clear of obstacles

WARM-UP ACTIVITIES (5-7 MINUTES)

1. Introduce the front support by demonstrating it (you or a student). Identify critical elements, and ask students to look for them as the support is demonstrated again. Students should then practice in self space. The students should hold the support until the teacher has seen every student. Use this procedure to introduce the rear and side supports.

2. Introduce the game "Find the support." Gather students and inform them that they are going to play a game called "Find the support." Students may walk, run, or skip within a defined area (use cones to mark the area). When you name a support, the students must quickly assume that support. The goal is to have every student quickly and correctly assume the position. During the game assess the students using the skills checklist.

REVIEW AND ASSESS (14 MINUTES)

Balances

1. Introduce each of the balances by naming it ("This is a T-stand."), demonstrating it (you or a student), identifying the critical elements ("Did you see how my arms were up like an airplane and my body was straight?"), and demonstrate again with students looking for the critical elements ("I'm going to demonstrate the T-stand again. Let's see if you can tell me if I am doing it correctly."). You might make a mistake or two (e.g., bent arms) in order to have students discriminate errors. Then let the students practice in self space.

2. Use this procedure for standing tall, T-stand, landing shape, pike, and tuck sit.

3. Next, play "Balance 1-2-3." The teacher says the name of the balance (e.g., T-stand), then "Balance 1-2-3" representing three seconds. Go through each balance several times using this game and assess all the students on each skill.

Rotations

1. Review the back rocker by demonstrating it. Identify critical elements and demonstrate it again asking students to look for the critical elements. Then allow students to practice it in self space 6 to 10 times. Look for common errors and bring the class together to review the common errors and critical elements.

2. Use the same procedure for the back rocker to stand and from stand to back rocker. Assess each skill as students practice.

3. Review the full log rolls in the same manner. Arrange the class so they are all facing the same way, lying on their backs with approximately three or four feet between each student (use rows and columns for organization). Have the class roll in the same direction onto their backs, then roll back the other direction.

4. Next begin the roll with students lying on their stomachs and repeat the activity. During this time assess student performance.

2-2

The following tasks should be accomplished in this lesson:

Review and Assess

Review and assess any skills or students not covered in lesson 1.

New Skills

Balances

Straddle sit
Knee scale
Straddle stand
Shoulder-feet balance

Supports

Tuck to front support
Front support to tuck
Front support to straddle stand
Straddle stand to front support

Rotations

Forward roll on mat to sit

Equipment

Mats
Open area clear of obstacles

WARM-UP ACTIVITIES (3-5 MINUTES)

Play the games "Find the support" and "Balance 1-2-3" (see lesson 1).

REVIEW (5 MINUTES)

Review and assess any skills or students not covered in lesson 1.

NEW SKILLS (20 MINUTES)

Balances

1. Introduce the straddle sit by demonstrating it (you or a student). Identify critical elements, and ask students to look for them as the straddle sit is demonstrated again. Students should then practice in self space.

2. Use this procedure (demonstrate, review critical elements, demonstrate, and practice) to introduce the knee scale, straddle stand, and shoulder-feet balance.

Supports

Introduce the following skills individually as you did with the balances (demonstrate, review critical elements, demonstrate, and practice): tuck to front support, front support to tuck, front support to straddle stand, and straddle stand to front support.

Rotations

1. Introduce the forward roll on mat to sit by reviewing the back rocker and performing the back rocker to sit on the floor four or five times for each student.

2. Next, demonstrate the roll (you or a student), identify critical elements, and ask students to look for them as the skill is demonstrated again. Be sure to emphasize hand placement and head tuck. Students should then practice in self space. Students should perform this task at least 10 times with rest between each attempt. You can best achieve this if you have a large group and few mats by alternating practices between two or three students sharing one mat.

2-3

The following tasks should be accomplished in this lesson:

Review

Balances

Straddle sit
Knee scale
Straddle stand
Shoulder-feet balance

Supports

Tuck to front support
Front support to tuck
Front support to straddle stand
Straddle stand to front support

Rotations

Forward roll on mat to sit

New Skills

Rotations

Partner log rolls

Equipment

Mats
Open area clear of obstacles

WARM-UP ACTIVITIES (5 MINUTES)

Play "Balance 1-2-3" and review balances.

REVIEW (14 MINUTES)

Balances

1. Review the straddle sit by asking the class to demonstrate it. Review and correct critical elements.

2. Use this procedure to review the knee scale, straddle stand, and shoulder-feet balance. Allow at least six opportunities per skill for practice.

Supports

In a similar manner, review the supports tuck to front support, front support to tuck, front support to straddle stand, and straddle stand to front support.

Rotations

Review the forward roll on mat to sit as you introduced it in lesson 2. Ask the class to perform the back rocker and the back rocker to sit on the floor four or five times. Next, demonstrate the roll, identify critical elements, and ask students to look for them as the skill is demonstrated again. Allow at least 10 opportunities (preferably 15 or more) for practice. Correct errors as you see them occur. Alternate practice trials between students.

NEW SKILLS (10 MINUTES)

Rotations

1. Introduce the partner log rolls by reviewing the full log rolls and having the class perform a few full log rolls. Divide the class into pairs of students.

2. Next, demonstrate the partner log rolls using two students. Identify critical elements, and arrange the class so they are all rolling in the same direction (nominate a wall or side to roll toward). Make the task a mini-competition to see which pairs can roll without breaking form (bending legs or arms or letting go of hands). The goal is for each pair to roll together without breaking form. Note it is not a race but rather a form and neatness competition.

2-4

The following tasks should be accomplished in this lesson:

Assess

Balances

Straddle sit
Knee scale
Straddle stand
Shoulder-feet balance

Rotations

Forward roll on mat to sit

Review

Rotations

Partner log rolls

Supports

Tuck to front support
Front support to tuck
Front support to straddle stand
Straddle stand to front support

New Skills

Rotations

Forward roll down incline to tuck
Back rocker with hand touch

Equipment

Mats
Open area clear of obstacles
Inclines to roll down, such as a triangular, wedge-shaped foam mat or two mats on top of a springboard

WARM-UP ACTIVITIES (5-6 MINUTES)

Play "Balance 1-2-3" using the skills straddle sit, knee scale, straddle stand, and shoulder-feet balance. Using the skills checklist, assess students on these skills as they play the game.

ASSESS (DURING NEW SKILLS)

Assess the forward roll on mat to sit during the rotations circuit described in the new skills section.

REVIEW (5-6 MINUTES)

Supports

Have the class perform the supports tuck to front support, front support to tuck, front support to straddle stand, and straddle stand to front support. Have students practice these skills at least five times each.

Rotations

Review the partner log rolls and have the class perform this skill several times in each direction. Remind the class of the goal for each pair to roll together without breaking form.

NEW SKILLS (12 MINUTES)

Rotations

1. Instruct the class as a group to touch hands in the back rocker. While the class practices, walk around and correct errors. The key task in this skill is to keep the hands by the ears and to make sure that the palms touch the floor (or very near it) as the student rocks backward.

2. Next make a circuit of six or eight stations (per 20 students). Use four skills in the circuit: forward roll on mat to sit, forward roll down incline to tuck, back rocker with hand touch, and back rocker to stand. Create one or two stations per skill, depending on the number of students in your class and how many inclines you have. Seat the class on the side of the circuit. Describe and demonstrate what they will do at each station (particularly the forward roll down incline to tuck).

Then have a student demonstrate the whole circuit without stopping. Designate class members, three or four per station, and give them 30 to 40 seconds at each station before they move to the next station. Once the students have been through the station, begin assessment of forward roll on mat to sit and correct any errors in the skills they are performing. You will use this circuit in the remaining lessons of this unit in different forms.

Hint: One way to control the 30- to 40-second rotation is to make a cassette tape that plays music for 5 seconds (the rotation from station to station) and is silent for 40 seconds (or the reverse). The sequence 40 + 5 should repeat itself 12 to 14 times, giving you a 10 minute continuous sequence.

2-5

The following tasks should be accomplished in this lesson:

Assess

Supports

Tuck to front support
Front support to tuck
Front support to straddle stand
Straddle stand to front support

Review

Rotations

Forward roll on mat to sit
Forward roll down incline to tuck
Back rocker with hand touch

Balances

Straddle sit
Knee scale
Straddle stand
Shoulder-feet balance

New Skills

Springing and Landing

Jump over a hoop
Jump backward into a hoop
Frog jump (feet together)
Frog jump (feet apart)
Crab walk

Equipment

Mats
Open area clear of obstacles
Hoops (one per child) or draw circles using
    chalk or masking tape
Inclines

WARM-UP ACTIVITIES (3-5 MINUTES)

Play "Balance 1-2-3" using the skills straddle sit, knee scale, straddle stand, and shoulder-feet balance.

ASSESS (6 MINUTES)

Assess the supports tuck to front support, front support to tuck, front support to straddle stand, and straddle stand to front support, using the skills checklist. Have students practice the skills, and during the practice assess students on each skill.

REVIEW (8 MINUTES)

Rotations

Reintroduce the circuit used in the previous lesson. Using a circuit of six or eight stations (per 20 students), review the forward roll on mat to sit, forward roll down incline to tuck, back rocker with hand touch, and back rocker to stand (see lesson 4 for details). As students move through the circuit, correct errors and provide individual assistance.

NEW SKILLS (10 MINUTES)

Springing and Landing

1. Review the landing shape and have the class practice jumping and landing in the landing shape in self space.

2. Next, place hoops around the floor. State the critical elements and demonstrate how to perform the jump over a hoop. A perfect jump is one in which the student lands and is immediately steady (no falls, stumbles, or steps). Have students practice the task six times and correct errors. Pay particular attention to the arm swing. Using the same hoops, demonstrate the jump backward into a hoop. State the critical elements and allow 6 to 10 opportunities to practice.

3. You can best introduce the skills frog jump (feet together), frog jump (feet apart), and crab walk by teaching one child the skill and having him or her demonstrate it to the class. Set the direction you want the students to move (e.g., in a circle) and have them frog jump. Once everyone is moving, correct errors. It is easier to demonstrate this skill and have students watch and copy like "Follow the leader" than it is to explain it. Watch for students who jump simultaneously with their hands and their feet instead of allowing their feet to land before moving their hands. Tell students to keep their distance (one or two feet) from other students to avoid getting kicked accidentally.

2-6

The following tasks should be accomplished in this lesson:

Review

Springing and Landing

Jump over a hoop
Jump backward into a hoop
Frog jump (feet together)
Frog jump (feet apart)
Crab walk

Rotations

Forward roll on mat to sit
Forward roll down incline to tuck
Back rocker with hand touch
Back rocker to stand
Partner log rolls

Balances

Straddle sit
Knee scale
Straddle stand
Shoulder-feet balance

Supports

Tuck to front support
Front support to tuck
Front support to straddle stand
Straddle stand to front support

Equipment

Mats
Open area clear of obstacles
Hoops
Incline

WARM-UP ACTIVITIES (3-5 MINUTES)

Play "Balance 1-2-3" using the skills straddle sit, knee scale, straddle stand, and shoulder-feet balance.

REVIEW (24 MINUTES)

Supports

Review the supports tuck to front support, front support to tuck, front support to straddle stand, and straddle stand to front support.

Rotations

Reintroduce the circuit used in lesson 4 to review the forward roll on mat to sit, forward roll down incline to tuck, back rocker with hand touch, and back rocker to stand. As students move through the circuit, correct errors and provide individual assistance.

Springing and Landing

1. Review the landing shape and have the class practice jumping and landing in the landing shape in self space.

2. Next, review the jump over a hoop, then the jump backward into a hoop. Option: You might like to include the skills as one of the stations in the previous circuit.

Springing and Landing

Review frog jump (feet apart), frog jump (feet together), and the crab walk. As students practice, correct errors.

Rotations

Review the partner log rolls. Divide the class into pairs and arrange the students so they will all roll in the same direction. Begin with the students lying on their stomachs. Students should practice rolling in both directions.

2-7

The following tasks should be accomplished in this lesson:

Assess

Rotations

Forward roll down incline to tuck
Back rocker with hand touch
Partner log rolls

Springing and Landing

Jump over a hoop
Jump backward into a hoop
Frog jump (feet together)
Frog jump (feet apart)
Crab walk

Review

Rotations

Forward roll on mat to sit

Balances

Straddle sit
Knee scale
Straddle stand
Shoulder-feet balance

Supports

Tuck to front support
Front support to tuck
Front support to straddle stand
Straddle stand to front support

Equipment

Mats
Open area clear of obstacles
Hoops
Incline

WARM-UP ACTIVITIES (3-5 MINUTES)

Play "Balance 1-2-3" using the skills straddle sit, knee scale, straddle stand, and shoulder-feet balance.

ASSESS (8 MINUTES)

Rotations

1. Assess the partner log rolls as students practice it. Have the class roll in the same direction onto their backs, then roll back in the other direction. Assess the forward roll down incline to tuck and the back rocker with hand touch, either in the group or as part of the circuit described in the review section.

Springing and Landing

1. In a similar manner to the partner log rolls, assess frog jump (feet apart), frog jump (feet together), and the crab walk as students practice them.
2. You can assess jump over a hoop, then jump backward into a hoop as part of the following circuit.

REVIEW (16 MINUTES)

Supports

Review the supports tuck to front support, front support to tuck, front support to straddle stand, and straddle stand to front support.

Rotations

Reintroduce the circuit used in the previous lessons. Using a circuit of six or eight stations (per 20 students), review the forward roll on mat to sit, forward roll down incline to tuck, back rocker with hand touch, and back rocker to stand. Create one or two stations per skill depending on the number of students in your class and how many inclines you have (or can make). Students should now know the circuit (depending when your last lesson occurred), so a simple description may suffice; if not, use a student to demonstrate. As students move through the circuit, you can assess their performance of the forward roll down incline to tuck and the back rocker with hand touch.

3-1

The following tasks should be accomplished in this lesson:

Review and Assess

Supports

Tuck to front support
Front support to tuck
Front support to straddle stand
Straddle stand to front support

Rotations

Back rocker with hand touch
Forward roll on mat to sit
Forward roll down incline to tuck

New Skill

Game "Front support tag"

Equipment

Mats
Open area clear of obstacles
Inclines to roll down, such as a triangular, wedge-shaped foam mat or two mats on top of a springboard

WARM-UP ACTIVITIES (5-7 MINUTES)

Play the game "Front support tag." This is a typical tag game. Define the boundaries of the game, nominate one to three students to tag the rest of the class (rotate students into and out of this role). When tagged, a student assumes a front support position. To be freed, a student who is free must crawl under a tagged student (from the side).

REVIEW AND ASSESS (20 MINUTES)

Supports

Introduce each support skill individually (tuck to front support, front support to tuck, front support to straddle stand, and straddle stand to front support) by demonstrating it. Identify critical elements, and ask students to look for them as the skill is demonstrated again. Students should then practice in self space. The students should practice the skill until the teacher has assessed every student.

Rotations

1. Make a circuit of six or eight stations (per 20 students). Use four skills in the circuit: the forward roll on mat to sit, forward roll down incline to tuck, back rocker with hand touch, and back rocker to stand. Create one or two stations per skill, depending on the number of students in your class and how many inclines you have (or can make). Seat the class on the side of the circuit, and describe and demonstrate what they will do at each station. Then have a student demonstrate the whole circuit without stopping.

2. Designate class members (three or four per station) and give them 30 to 40 seconds at each station before they move to the next station. Once the students have been through the station, begin assessment of forward roll on mat to sit or correct any errors in the skills being performed. You will use this circuit in the remaining lessons of this unit in different forms.

Hint: One way to control the 30- to 40-second rotation is to make a cassette tape that plays music for 5 seconds (the rotation from station to station) and is silent for 40 seconds (or the reverse). The sequence 40 + 5 should repeat itself 12 to 14 times, giving you a 10 minute continuous sequence. Correct and assess students during practice.

3-2

The following tasks should be accomplished in this lesson:

Review

Rotations

Forward roll on mat to sit
Forward roll down incline to tuck
Back rocker with hand touch

New skills

Balances

Shoulder balance
Tripod balance

Rotations

Forward roll down incline to stand
Cartwheel weight transfer along bench

Equipment

Mats
Open area clear of obstacles
Inclines to roll down
Benches or raised platform (not more than 18 inches high)

WARM-UP ACTIVITIES (3-5 MINUTES)

Play the game "Front support tag" (see lesson 1).

REVIEW (5 MINUTES)

Rotations

Make a circuit of six or eight stations (per 20 students) with the four skills, forward roll on mat to sit, forward roll down incline to tuck, back rocker with hand touch, and back rocker to stand, as described in lesson 1. Once the students have been through the station, correct any errors in the skills they are performing.

NEW SKILLS (18-20 MINUTES)

Balances

1. Introduce the tripod balance using three progressions. First, demonstrate how to place the head and hands in a triangle. Next, have students practice lifting one leg at a time up onto the forearm (one leg always remains on the floor). When students can do this, introduce the whole skill by having a student demonstrate it. Identify the critical elements, and demonstrate again with students looking for the critical elements. Allow at least five or six minutes of practice time for this skill. While students rest between attempts, have them watch their partners and provide feedback on the placement of the head and hands.

2. Introduce the shoulder balance in a similar manner by demonstrating and identifying the critical elements.

Rotations

1. Introduce the forward roll down incline to stand by having a student demonstrate it. Identify critical elements, but stress that this skill is the same as the forward roll down incline to tuck except the student stands up instead of staying tucked.

2. Once you finish the demonstration, nominate a new station (if you have two or more inclines) in the existing circuit for the forward roll down incline to stand (remove the forward roll down incline to tuck from the circuit).

3. Introduce the cartwheel weight transfer along bench. Emphasize that in this skill the goal is to transfer weight from one side of the bench to the other. Identify the one-two action of the legs—that the leg closest to the bench is moved over the bench followed by the other leg. Have the students repeat the one-two action three or four times.

3-3

The following tasks should be accomplished in this lesson:

Balances

Shoulder balance
Tripod balance

Rotations

Forward roll down incline to stand
Forward roll on mat to sit
Forward roll down incline to tuck
Back rocker with hand touch

New Skills

Supports

Front support change to rear support

Rotations

Backward roll down incline to tuck
Sit and spin
Jump, twist, and freeze

Springing and Landing

Jump from a low height with straight shape

Equipment

Mats
Open area clear of obstacles
Benches or raised platforms (one or two feet high and sturdy enough for children to jump from)
Inclines

WARM-UP ACTIVITIES (5-7 MINUTES)

Play the game "Front support tag." Review the rear and side supports (see unit 1), and play the variations "Rear support tag" and "Side support tag."

REVIEW (10 MINUTES)

Balances

1. Review the shoulder balance. Pair students up. Have a student demonstrate the shoulder balance and identify the critical elements. Let the students practice in self space.

2. When reviewing the tripod balance, use the three progressions from the previous lesson. First, demonstrate how to place the head and hands in a triangle (see drills in chapter 2). Next, have students practice lifting one leg at a time up onto the forearm (one leg always remains on the floor). When students can do this, introduce the whole skill by having a student demonstrate it. Identify the critical elements, and demonstrate again with students looking for the critical elements.

Rotations

1. Make a circuit of six or eight stations (per 20 students) with the skills forward roll on mat to sit, forward roll down incline to tuck, back rocker with hand touch, and forward roll down incline to stand as described in lesson 2.

2. Once the students have been through the station, begin review of forward roll on mat to sit or correct any errors in the skills they are performing.

NEW SKILLS (10 MINUTES)

Supports

Introduce the front support change to rear support. Have a student demonstrate the front support starting position, the transition, and the rear support ending position. Identify the critical element—lifting one hand off the floor and turning over to rear support.

Rotations

1. Introduce the backward roll down incline to tuck by having a student demonstrate it. Demonstrate the skill and identify critical elements. Then demonstrate with students observing the critical elements.

2. Once you finish the demonstration, nominate a new station (if you have two or more inclines) in the existing circuit for the forward roll down incline to stand (remove the forward roll down incline to tuck from the circuit).

3. Introduce the sit and spin. Have a student demonstrate it and identify critical elements.

4. Introduce the jump, twist and freeze by having a student demonstrate it. Identify the critical elements of the skill.

Springing and Landing

Introduce jump from a low height with straight shape by having a student demonstrate it; then identify the critical elements. Have the class practice in self space; then add this skill to the existing circuit by creating a station with a raised platform to jump from. Make sure you emphasize the landing shape (i.e., landing with legs bent and arms stretched out).

3-4

The following tasks should be accomplished in this lesson:

Assess

Rotations

Forward roll down incline to stand

Springing and Landing

Jump from a low height with straight shape

Review

Supports

Front support change to rear support

Rotations

Cartwheel weight transfer along bench
Backward roll down incline to tuck
Sit and spin
Jump, twist, and freeze

Balances

Shoulder balance
Tripod balance

New Skills

Rotations

Forward roll on mat to stand
Cartwheel over an inclined rope

Equipment

Mats
Open area clear of obstacles
Benches or raised platforms
Inclines
Ropes

WARM-UP ACTIVITIES (5 MINUTES)

Play the games "Front support tag," "Rear support tag," and "Side support tag."

REVIEW (12 MINUTES)

Balances

Review the shoulder balance and the tripod balance. Pair students up. If students can perform the shoulder balance without assistance, allow them to do so. If students can perform the tripod balance, spend little if any time on the progressions. If students cannot perform the tripod balance, spend the majority of the time on the progressions. Check to see if the hands and head form a triangle and if the student is able to lift each leg off the floor and hold it up.

Rotations

Using the circuit developed in lesson 3, set up stations to incorporate each of the following skills: backward roll down incline to tuck; cartwheel weight transfer along bench; sit and spin; and jump, twist, and freeze.

ASSESS (DURING REVIEW CIRCUIT)

Rotations

Add the skill forward roll down incline to stand to the review circuit, and assess students individually as they attempt the skill.

Springing and Landing

Create a station in the circuit for jump from a low height with straight shape, and assess students individually as they perform it.

NEW SKILLS (12 MINUTES)

Rotations

1. Introduce the forward roll on mat to stand by having a student demonstrate the forward roll down incline to stand. Next, ask the student to demonstrate the forward roll on mat to stand. Critical elements remain the same, so you should spend little effort here, but develop a generalization of skill from the incline to the mat. Those students who can perform this skill need not perform the skill down the incline (thus freeing the incline for backward rolls).

2. Demonstrate the cartwheel over an inclined rope. Then identify the critical elements. Emphasize hand placement and leg action. Next, perform the skill again so the students may observe the critical elements. Include this task either as part of the original circuit or as a separate circuit of six to nine stations with two or three children at each station. Children do not rotate from the station, but take turns performing the skill at one station.

3-5

The following tasks should be accomplished in this lesson:

Assess

Balances

Shoulder balance
Tripod balance

Supports

Front support change to rear support

Review

Rotations

Forward roll down incline to stand
Forward roll on mat to stand
Cartwheel over an inclined rope
Cartwheel weight transfer along bench
Backward roll down incline to tuck

Springing and Landing

Jump from a low height with straight shape

New Skills

Balances

Counterbalances

Springing and Landing

Seal walk
Lame monkey walk

Equipment

Mats
Open area clear of obstacles
Benches or raised platforms
Inclines
Ropes
Counterbalance task cards from appendix A

WARM-UP ACTIVITIES (8 MINUTES)

To introduce counterbalances, place students into pairs. Explain the concept of a seesaw: "Two people of different heights and weights can balance at each end, and this is called a counterbalance. For example two friends of different sizes who sit at each end of the seesaw could find a balance. The seesaw might not be level. It might be inclined, but a balance can be obtained. This exercise is about two partners finding a balance." (See appendix A for task cards.) Introduce each balance separately. Name it, state the steps (critical elements listed on each task card), and let students practice it.

REVIEW (5 MINUTES)

Set up a circuit using the following rotation and springing and landing skills: forward roll down incline to stand, forward roll on mat to stand, cartwheel weight transfer along bench, backward roll down incline to tuck, cartwheel over an inclined rope, and jump from a low height with straight shape.

ASSESS (10 MINUTES)

Add the following balances and supports to the review circuit: shoulder balance, tripod balance, and front support change to rear support. Assess students as they rotate through the circuit.

NEW SKILLS (5 MINUTES)

Springing and Landing

1. Introduce the seal walk by having a student demonstrate the skill. Identify critical elements and challenge the class to see if they can keep their legs straight and together throughout the seal walk. Have a student demonstrate again and ask the class to observe the performance. Then let the class practice in self space.

2. Use the same procedure to introduce the lame monkey walk. It helps to tell the students that the monkey has a broken leg and it must remain straight. The action of the lame monkey walk is similar to the kick up to one-leg handstand, except the top leg doesn't raise as high and the body moves forward with each kick.

3-6

The following tasks should be accomplished in this lesson:

Assess

Rotations

Sit and spin
Jump, twist, and freeze
Cartwheel weight transfer along bench
Cartwheel over an inclined rope

Review

Rotations

Forward roll down incline to stand
Forward roll on mat to stand
Backward roll down incline to tuck

Springing and Landing

Jump from a low height with straight shape
Seal walk
Lame monkey walk

Supports

Front support change to rear support

Balances

Counterbalances
Shoulder balance
Tripod balance

Equipment

Mats
Open area clear of obstacles
Benches or raised platforms
Inclines
Ropes
Counterbalance task cards

WARM-UP ACTIVITIES (7 MINUTES)

Review counterbalances by showing the class the counterbalance task cards. Place these cards in a circuit and give students (in pairs) 30 seconds at each station.

REVIEW (10 MINUTES)

Set up a circuit using the following skills: shoulder balance, tripod balance, forward roll down incline to stand, forward roll on mat to stand, backward roll down incline to tuck, and jumping from a low height with straight shape.

ASSESS (7 MINUTES)

Assess the following rotations: cartwheel weight transfer along bench; cartwheel over an inclined rope; sit and spin; and jump, twist, and freeze. Include these skills in the previous circuit or assess them individually.

3-7

The following tasks should be accomplished in this lesson:

Assess

Springing and Landing
Seal walk
Lame monkey walk

Rotations
Forward roll on mat to stand
Backward roll down incline to tuck

Balances
Counterbalances

Review

Rotations
Sit and spin
Jump, twist, and freeze
Cartwheel weight transfer along bench
Cartwheel over an inclined rope
Forward roll down incline to stand

Springing and Landing
Jump from a low height with straight shape

Balances
Shoulder balance
Tripod balance

Equipment
Mats
Open area clear of obstacles
Benches or raised platforms
Inclines
Ropes
Counterbalance task cards

WARM-UP ACTIVITIES (10 MINUTES)

Set up the circuit used in lesson 6 for the counterbalance task cards. Assess students as they rotate through the stations. Note that you need only assess two of the counterbalances per student. These may be the same for the class or different for each couple, depending on your assessment goals.

REVIEW (10 MINUTES)

Set up a circuit using the following skills: shoulder balance; tripod balance; cartwheel weight transfer along bench; cartwheel over an inclined rope; sit and spin; jump, twist, and freeze; forward roll down incline to stand; and jump from a low height with straight shape.

ASSESS (5 MINUTES)

Include forward roll on mat to stand and backward roll down incline to tuck in the previous circuit, or assess them individually. Do likewise with seal walk and lame monkey walk. Counterbalances are assessed during warm-up activities.

4-1

The following tasks should be accomplished in this lesson:

Review and Assess

Balances

Counterbalances

Rotations

Forward roll down incline to stand
Backward roll down incline to tuck
Cartwheel weight transfer along bench

Springing and Landing

Seal walk

Equipment

Mats
Open area clear of obstacles
Benches or raised platforms
Inclines to roll down, such as a triangular, wedge-shaped foam mat or two mats on top of a springboard
Counterbalance task cards

WARM-UP ACTIVITIES (10 MINUTES)

As warm-up activities, review counterbalances using task cards from appendix A.

REVIEW AND ASSESS (16 MINUTES)

Springing and Landing

Review the seal walk by having a student demonstrate the skill. Identify critical elements and challenge the class to see if they can keep their legs straight and together throughout the seal walk. Have a student demonstrate again and ask the class to observe the performance. Then let the class practice in self space. Review the landing by having a student demonstrate it, then identify the critical elements. Have the class practice in self space, then add this skill to the existing circuit by creating a station with a raised platform to jump off. Make sure you emphasize the landing shape (i.e., landing with legs bent and arms stretched out).

Rotations

Make a circuit of six stations (per 20 students), using the skills forward roll down incline to stand, backward roll down incline to tuck, and cartwheel weight transfer along bench. Create one or two stations per skill depending on the number of

students in your class and how many inclines you have (or can make). Seat the class on the side of the circuit, and describe and demonstrate what they will do at each station. Then have a student demonstrate the whole circuit without stopping. Designate class members (three or four per station) and give them 30 to 40 seconds at each station before they move to the next station.

Hint 1: One way to control the 30- to 40-second rotation is to make a cassette tape that plays music for 5 seconds (the rotation from station to station) and is silent for 40 seconds (or the reverse). The sequence 40 + 5 should repeat itself 12 to 14 times, giving you a 10 minute continuous sequence. Correct and assess students during practice.

Hint 2: If you don't have enough inclines, make more rope stations or add the earlier skills to the circuit (seal walk, counterbalances, and landing) to increase opportunities to practice and lessen waiting.

4-2

The following tasks should be accomplished in this lesson:

Review

Balances

Counterbalances

New Skills

Rotations

Forward roll on mat to stand

Balances

Headstand

Springing and Landing

Jump from a low height with tuck shape
Lame monkey walk
Frog jump (feet apart)
Frog jump (feet together)

Equipment

Mats
Open area clear of obstacles
Benches or raised platforms
Counterbalance task cards

WARM-UP ACTIVITIES (5-7 MINUTES)

Review counterbalances by showing the class the counterbalance task cards. Place these cards in a circuit and give students (in pairs) 30 seconds at each station to demonstrate the counterbalance (you may have several couples at each station). Rotate through all stations.

NEW SKILLS (21 MINUTES)

Rotations

Introduce the forward roll on mat to stand by having a student demonstrate it. Identify critical elements and ask the class to observe the skill again, paying attention to the critical elements. Allocate students to mats and have students practice the forward roll on mat to stand.

Balances

1. Introduce the headstand using four progressions. First, demonstrate how to place the head and hands in a triangle.

2. Next, have students practice lifting one leg at a time into the air (one leg always remains on the floor). When students can do this, introduce the bent-leg headstand by asking students to gradually lift both feet off the floor while maintaining balance.

3. Finally, with students in pairs, have one student perform a one-leg headstand with the other student holding that leg at the calf. Then have the performing student lift the other leg up to join the extended leg. With each progression, have a student demonstrate it and identify the critical elements. Demonstrate again with students looking for the critical elements. Allow at least five or six minutes of practice time for this skill and for short rests (30 seconds) between attempts.

While students rest between attempts, have them watch their partners and provide feedback on the placement of the head and hands. The goal is for no student to roll or fall forward or onto his back. *Therefore always use the assisting students when the headstand is performed.*

Springing and Landing

1. Introduce the lame monkey walk, frog jump (feet together), and frog jump (feet apart) by having a student demonstrate each one. Identify critical elements, then let students practice in self space. Be careful to allocate enough room to avoid students kicking each other accidentally, and have students follow the rule to stop moving if they get too close to others.

2. Introduce jump from a low height with tuck shape by having a student demonstrate it; then identify the critical elements. Have the class practice in self space on the floor without jumping from height. Then use a low stage or benches to create the height, and let students practice this skill by jumping off the bench. Make sure you emphasize the landing shape (i.e., landing with legs bent and arms stretched out).

4-3

The following tasks should be accomplished in this lesson:

Review

Rotations

Forward roll on mat to stand

Balances

Headstand

Springing and Landing

Jump from a height with tuck shape
Lame monkey walk
Frog jump (feet apart)
Frog jump (feet together)

New Skills

Balances

Wall walk to handstand

Rotations

Backward roll down incline to stand
Cartwheel over an inclined rope
Minicartwheel over a bench

Equipment

Mats
Open area clear of obstacles
Benches or raised platforms
Inclines
Wall for students to walk up with their feet
Ropes
Counterbalance task cards
Chalk or tape

WARM-UP ACTIVITIES (5 MINUTES)

Set up the circuit as described in lesson 2, using the counterbalance task cards. Place these cards in a circuit and give students (in pairs) 30 seconds at each station to demonstrate the counterbalance (you may have several couples at each station).

REVIEW (10 MINUTES)

Create a circuit with seven stations: *Station 1.* Lame monkey walk between cones spaced four to seven feet apart. *Station 2.* A low bench for jump from a low height with tuck shape. *Station 3.* Forward roll on mat to stand. *Station 4.* Frog jump (feet apart) between cones spaced four to seven feet apart. *Station 5.* Headstand where students practice lifting one leg at a time into the air (one leg always remains on the floor). Students lift each leg twice. *Station 6.* Frog jump (feet together) between cones spaced four to seven feet apart. *Station 7.* Headstand where students practice lifting one leg at a time into the air (repeat of station 5). Students lift each leg twice. Seat the class on the side of the circuit, and describe and demonstrate what they will do at each station. Then have a student demonstrate the whole circuit without stopping. Designate class members (three or four per station) and give them 30 to 40 seconds at each station before they move to the next station (consider using the musical tape described in unit 2 to control the rotation).

Balances

Review the headstand by grouping students in pairs. One student in the pair performs a one-leg headstand with the other student holding that leg at the calf. Then have the performing student lift the other leg up to join the extended leg. Allow each student at least five or six opportunities to practice this skill with a partner.

NEW SKILLS (12 MINUTES)

Rotations

1. Introduce the backward roll down incline to stand by having a student demonstrate it. Identify critical elements, and ask the class to observe the skill again, paying attention to the critical elements. Allocate students to inclines and have them practice performing backward roll down incline to stand. If there are not enough inclines, introduce this skill after both cartwheel skills and incorporate the three into a circuit with nine stations. Repeat each skill three times in the whole circuit. Introduce the cartwheel over an inclined rope by demonstrating, then stating the critical elements. Emphasize hand placement and leg action. Create a circuit of six to nine stations with an inclined rope at each station (use masking tape to attach it lightly to the wall and the floor). Place two or three children at each station. Children do not rotate from here, but take turns performing the skill at this assigned station.

2. Introduce minicartwheel over a bench in the same manner as the cartwheel over an inclined rope. Demonstrate, then identify the critical elements. Emphasize hand placement and leg action. Next, perform the skill again so the students may observe the critical elements. If you have enough benches (no higher than 18 inches) to create six to nine stations, then duplicate the arrangement used for the cartwheel over an inclined rope drill. Place two or three children at each station. Children do not rotate from here, but take turns performing the skill at this assigned station. If you do not have enough stations, you might create a composite circuit of inclined ropes and benches, and have students rotate from one station to another.

Balances

Introduce the wall walk to handstand. As explained in the drill and progressions, have students systematically walk up the wall to each of the four lines. Be careful that students do not move too close to the wall. Some students may not feel comfortable going above the second or third line on the first few attempts. Focus on the competency of walking up and walking down the wall rather than how high they can walk.

4-4

The following tasks should be accomplished in this lesson:

Assess

Rotations

Forward roll on mat to stand

Springing and Landing

Jump from a low height with tuck shape
Lame monkey walk
Frog jump (feet apart)
Frog jump (feet together)

Review

Balances

Wall walk to handstand
Headstand

Rotations

Backward roll down incline to stand
Cartwheel over an inclined rope
Minicartwheel over a bench

Equipment

Mats
Open area clear of obstacles
Benches or raised platforms
Inclines
Wall
Ropes
Chalk or tape

WARM-UP ACTIVITIES (10 MINUTES)

Have students perform the lame monkey walk, frog jump (feet apart), and frog jump (feet together) as a warm-up activity. Deal with each skill separately and assess each student's performance.

REVIEW (17 MINUTES)

1. Set up a circuit with six stations: *Station 1.* Backward roll down incline to stand. *Station 2.* A low bench for jump from a low height with tuck shape. *Station 3.* Forward roll on mat to stand. *Station 4.* Headstand where students practice lifting one leg at a time into the air (one leg always remains on the floor). Students lift each leg twice. *Station 5.* Wall walk to handstand. *Station 6.* Headstand where students in pairs assist each other, holding the legs at the calves. Seat the class on the side of the circuit, and describe and demonstrate what they will do at each station. Then have a student demonstrate the whole circuit without stopping. Designate class members (three or four per station) and give them 30 to 40 seconds at each station before they move to the next station (consider using the musical tape described in unit 2 to control the rotation).

2. During this circuit, correct errors in the wall walk to handstand, the headstand, and the backward roll down incline to stand. Assess the forward roll on mat to stand and jump from a low height with tuck shape.

3. Once this circuit is complete, remove the skills from stations 2 and 5 and substitute minicartwheel over a bench and cartwheel over an inclined rope. Then continue with the circuit. The focus in this circuit should be on correcting performance errors.

4-5

The following tasks should be accomplished in this lesson:

Assess

Rotations

Backward roll down incline to stand
Cartwheel over an inclined rope

Review

Balances

Wall walk to handstand
Headstand

Rotations

Minicartwheel over a bench
Forward roll on mat to stand

Springing and Landing

Jump from a low height with tuck shape
Lame monkey walk
Frog jump (feet apart)
Frog jump (feet together)

New Skills

Rotations

Backward roll on mat to stand

Equipment

Mats
Open area clear of obstacles
Benches or raised platforms
Inclines
Wall
Ropes
Chalk or tape

WARM-UP ACTIVITIES (8 MINUTES)

Have students perform the lame monkey walk, frog jump (feet apart), and frog jump (feet together) as a warm-up activity. Review each skill separately.

REVIEW (12 MINUTES)

1. Set up a circuit with six stations: *Station 1.* Backward roll down incline to stand. *Station 2.* A low bench for jump from a height with tuck shape. *Station 3.* Forward roll on mat to stand. *Station 4.* Headstand where students practice lifting one leg at a time into the air (one leg always remains on the floor). Students lift each leg twice. *Station 5.* Wall walk to handstand. *Station 6.* Headstand where students in pairs assist each other, holding the legs at the calves. Seat the class on the side of the circuit, and describe and demonstrate what they will do at each station. Then have a student demonstrate the whole circuit without stopping. Designate class members (three or four per station) and give them 30 to 40 seconds at each station before they move to the next station (consider using the musical tape described in unit 2 to control the rotation).

2. During this circuit, correct errors in the wall walk to handstand, the headstand, and the backward roll down incline to stand. Assess the backward roll down incline to stand.

3. Once the assessment is complete, remove the skills from stations 2, 5, and 7 and substitute minicartwheel over a bench, cartwheel over an inclined rope, and introduce the skill backward roll on mat to stand for station 5. Then continue with the circuit. Assess the cartwheel over an inclined rope during this time. The focus in this circuit should be on correcting errors.

NEW SKILLS (5 MINUTES)

Rotations

Introduce the backward roll on mat to stand in the existing circuit by first having a student demonstrate the backward roll down incline to stand. Next, ask the student to demonstrate backward roll on mat to stand. Critical elements remain the same, so you should spend little effort here, but develop a generalization of skill from the incline to the mat.

4-6

The following tasks should be accomplished in this lesson:

Assess

Balances

Headstand

Rotations

Minicartwheel over a bench

Review

Balances

Wall walk to handstand

Rotations

Backward roll on mat to stand
Forward roll on mat to stand
Backward roll down incline to stand
Cartwheel over an inclined rope

Springing and Landing

Jump from a low height with tuck shape
Lame monkey walk
Frog jump (feet apart)
Frog jump (feet together)

Equipment

Mats
Open area clear of obstacles
Benches or raised platforms
Inclines
Wall
Ropes
Chalk or tape

WARM-UP ACTIVITIES (5 MINUTES)

Have students perform the lame monkey walk, frog jump (feet apart), and frog jump (feet together) as a warm-up activity. Review each skill separately.

REVIEW (15 MINUTES)

1. Set up a circuit with seven stations: *Station 1.* Backward roll down incline to stand. *Station 2.* A low bench for jump from a low height with tuck shape. *Station 3.* Forward roll on mat to stand. *Station 4.* Headstand where students practice lifting one leg at a time into the air (one leg always remains on the floor). Students lift each leg twice. *Station 5.* Wall walk to handstand. *Station 6.* Jump from a low height with a tuck shape. *Station 7.* Headstand where students in pairs assist each other, holding the legs at the calves. Seat the class on the side of the circuit, and describe and demonstrate what they will do at each station. Then have a student demonstrate the whole circuit without stopping. Designate class members (three or four per station) and give them 30 to 40 seconds at each station before they move to the next station (consider using the musical tape described in unit 2 to control the rotation). The focus in this circuit should be on correcting performance errors.

2. After students have completed the circuit twice, remove the skills from stations 2, 5, and 7 and substitute minicartwheel over a bench, cartwheel over an inclined rope, and backward roll on mat to stand. Then continue with the circuit. Assess the minicartwheel over a bench during this second circuit.

ASSESS (5 MINUTES)

Balances

Have the class perform the headstand in pairs, one student assisting and one performing. Assess all students while they practice the headstand.

Note: Be careful not to require headstands longer than two to five seconds.

4-7

The following tasks should be accomplished in this lesson:

Assess

Balances
Wall walk to handstand

Rotations
Backward roll on mat to stand

Review

Balances
Headstand

Rotations
Minicartwheel over a bench
Forward roll on mat to stand
Backward roll down incline to stand
Cartwheel over an inclined rope

Springing and Landing
Jump from a low height with tuck shape
Lame monkey walk
Frog jump (feet apart)
Frog jump (feet together)

Equipment
Mats
Open area clear of obstacles
Benches or raised platforms
Inclines
Wall
Ropes
Chalk or tape

WARM-UP ACTIVITIES (5 MINUTES)

Have students perform the lame monkey walk, frog jump (feet apart), and frog jump (feet together) as a warm-up activity. Review each skill separately.

REVIEW (15 MINUTES)

1. Create a circuit with seven stations: *Station 1.* Backward roll down incline to stand. *Station 2.* Minicartwheel over a bench. *Station 3.* Forward roll on mat to stand. *Station 4.* Headstand where students practice lifting one leg at a time into the air (one leg always remains on the floor). Students lift each leg twice. *Station 5.* Wall walk to handstand. *Station 6.* Jump from a low height with a tuck shape. *Station 7.* Headstand where students in pairs assist each other, holding the legs at the calves. Seat the class on the side of the circuit, and describe and demonstrate what they will do at each station. Then have a student demonstrate the whole circuit without stopping. Designate class members (three or four per station) and give them 30 to 40 seconds at each station before they move to the next station (consider using the musical tape described in unit 2 to control the rotation). The focus in this circuit should be on correcting performance errors.

2. After students have completed the circuit twice, remove the skills from stations 5 and 7 and substitute cartwheel over an inclined rope and the backward roll on mat to stand. Continue with the circuit.

ASSESS (6 MINUTES)

Assess during the previous circuit the wall walk to handstand and backward roll on mat to stand.

5-1

The following tasks should be accomplished in this lesson:

Review and Assess

Rotations

Forward roll on mat to stand
Backward roll down incline to stand
Cartwheel over an inclined rope

Springing and Landing

Lame monkey walk
Frog jump (feet together)
Frog jump (feet apart)

Equipment

Mats
Open area clear of obstacles
Inclines to roll down, such as a triangular, wedge-shaped foam mat or two mats on top of a springboard
Ropes
Warm-up task cards from appendix A
Equipment for warm-up

WARM-UP ACTIVITIES (8-10 MINUTES)

Before the lesson, copy the warm-up task cards from appendix A and adhere them to a cardboard backing (laminating these will make the task cards more durable).

1. Place the task cards in a widely spaced circle where you are conducting the lesson.

2. Take the class from task card to task card, and explain what to do at each station. Choose one student to demonstrate each station. Each task card should have its own station with enough equipment (e.g., ropes) for at least four students to practice. Students can rotate through the circuit in one of two ways. They could rotate from station to station as the teacher directs (e.g., 30 seconds to practice and 5 seconds to transition), or they can rotate when they complete each task. Focus on the correct performance of this circuit, because you will use the same circuit for all lessons in this unit.

REVIEW AND ASSESS (15-17 MINUTES)

Springing and Landing

Introduce the lame monkey walk, frog jump (feet together), and frog jump (feet apart) by having a student demonstrate each one. Identify critical elements; then let students practice in self space. Be careful to allocate enough room to avoid students kicking each other accidentally, and have students follow the rule to stop moving if they get too close to another person.

Rotations

Create a circuit of five or six stations (per 20 students). Use three skills in the circuit: forward roll on mat to stand, backward roll down incline to stand, and cartwheel over an inclined rope. Create one or two stations per skill, depending on the number of students in your class and how many inclines you have (or can make). Seat the class on the side of the circuit, and describe (state critical elements) and demonstrate what they will do at each station. Designate class members (three or four per station) and give them one or two minutes at each station before they move to the next station. Correct student performance during practice. Students who have trouble with any of these skills should perform the earlier related skills (see scope and sequence chart for program).

5-2

The following tasks should be accomplished in this lesson:

New Skills

Supports

Wheelbarrow walk

Balances

Headstand

Springing and Landing

Jump from varied heights in star and tuck shapes
Frog jump uphill (feet apart)
Frog jump uphill (feet together)

Equipment

Mats
Open area clear of obstacles
Benches or raised platforms
Warm-up task cards
Equipment for warm-up

WARM-UP ACTIVITIES (5-7 MINUTES)

Review the warm-up task cards by explaining and demonstrating what to do at each station. Use the same station locations that you used in lesson 1.

NEW SKILLS (20 MINUTES)

Supports

1. Review front support (see unit 2 for details). Allow students several practice opportunities.

2. Review the seal walk (see unit 3 for details). Allow students one or two practice opportunities.

3. Introduce the wheelbarrow walk by stating, "The wheelbarrow walk is a seal walk without the need to drag your legs. Instead your partner holds your legs." Demonstrate the wheelbarrow walk (use two students). Identify critical elements, and point out that the person who is holding the legs of the performer must be careful to go very slowly. Have the class watch again. Then divide the class into pairs of similar weights. Specify the direction you want the students to wheelbarrow walk. Before starting practice, offer an award (special activity, recognition, etc.) to any pair of students who can perform the wheelbarrow walk *without either partner falling*. The award provides additional motivation for students who might otherwise be careless. Do not encourage students to race each other, as this can result in falls.

Balances

Introduce the headstand using four progressions. First, demonstrate how to place the head and hands in a triangle. Next, have students practice lifting one leg at a time into the air (one leg always remains on the floor). When students can do this, introduce the bent-leg headstand by asking students to gradually lift both feet off the floor while maintaining balance. Finally, with students in pairs, have one student perform a one-leg headstand with the other student holding that leg at the calf. Then have the performing student lift the other leg to join the extended leg. With each progression, have a student demonstrate it and identify the critical elements. Demonstrate again with students looking for the critical elements. Allow at least five or six minutes of practice time for this skill and for short rests (30 seconds) between attempts. While students rest between attempts, have them watch their partners and provide feedback on the placement of the head and hands. The goal is for no student to roll or fall forward or onto his back. *Therefore, always use the assisting students when the headstand is performed.*

Springing and Landing

1. Introduce jump from varied heights in star and tuck shapes by having a student demonstrate them; then identify the critical elements. Have the class practice in self space on the floor without jumping from height. Then use a low stage or benches to create different heights.

2. Let students practice this skill by jumping off the raised platform. Make sure you emphasize the landing shape (i.e., landing with legs bent and arms stretched out). This works best if you have several benches or a stage that many students can jump from simultaneously. Introduce the frog jump uphill (feet apart) and frog jump uphill (feet together) individually by having a student demonstrate each one. Identify critical elements; then let students practice in self space. Be careful to allocate enough room to avoid students kicking each other accidentally, and have students follow the rule to stop moving if they get too close to another person. Keep the height of the uphill platform between 12 and 18 inches.

5-3

The following tasks should be accomplished in this lesson:

Review

Supports

Wheelbarrow walk

Balances

Headstand

Springing and Landing

Jump from varied heights in star and tuck shapes
Frog jump uphill (feet apart)
Frog jump uphill (feet together)

New Skills

Balances

Wall walk to handstand

Rotations

Forward roll from three different positions
Backward roll on mat to stand

Equipment

Mats
Open area clear of obstacles
Benches or raised platforms
Wall for students to walk up with their feet
Warm-up task cards
Equipment for warm-up
Chalk or tape

WARM-UP ACTIVITIES (5-6 MINUTES)

By now the students should know the warm-up circuit. (Always use the same location for the stations and activities that you used in previous lessons.) If your class requires a review, do so by explaining and demonstrating what to do at each station.

REVIEW (8-10 MINUTES)

Supports

Review the wheelbarrow walk by demonstrating it (use two students). Identify critical elements, and point out that the person who is holding the legs of the performer must be careful to go very slowly. Have the class watch again, and divide the class into pairs of similar weights. Specify the direction you want the students to wheelbarrow walk. Before starting practice, offer an award (special activity, recognition, etc.) to any pair of students who can perform the wheelbarrow walk without either partner falling.

Balances

Review the headstand by grouping students in pairs. One of the students in the pair performs a one-leg headstand with the other student holding that leg at the calf. Then have the performing student lift the other leg to join the extended leg. Allow each student at least five or six opportunities to practice this skill with a partner.

Springing and Landing

1. Review the straight jump and land in self space by having a student demonstrate it;

then identify the critical elements. Have the class practice in self space on the floor without jumping from height. Then use a low stage or benches to create different heights. Let students practice this skill by jumping from the raised platform. Make sure you emphasize the landing shape (i.e., landing with legs bent and arms stretched out). This works best if you have several benches or a stage that many students can jump from simultaneously. Then practice jump from varied heights in star and tuck shapes.

2. Review frog jump uphill (feet apart) and frog jump uphill (feet together) individually by having a student demonstrate each one. Identify critical elements; then let students practice in self space. Be careful to allocate enough room to avoid students kicking each other accidentally, and have students follow the rule to stop moving if they get too close to another person. Keep the height of the uphill platform between 12 and 18 inches.

NEW SKILLS (12 MINUTES)

Balances

Introduce the wall walk to handstand as explained in chapter 2 by having students systematically walk up the wall to each of the four lines. Be careful that students do not move too close to the wall. Students may not feel comfortable going above the second or third line on the first few attempts. Focus on the competency of walking up and walking down the wall rather than how high they can walk.

Rotations

Introduce these skills by making a circuit of six stations (per 20 students): *Station 1.* Forward roll on mat to stand. *Station 2.* Backward roll on mat to stand. *Station 3.* Back rocker (see unit 1 for details). *Station 4.* Stork stand held for five seconds (see unit 1 for details). *Station 5.* Straddle stand held for five seconds (see unit 2 for details). *Station 6.* Knee scale held for five seconds (see unit 2 for details). Seat the class on the side of the circuit, and describe and demonstrate what they will do at each station. Then have a student demonstrate the whole circuit without stopping. Designate class members (three or four per station) and give them 30 to 40 seconds at each station before they move to the next station. Students should perform all skills on mats. Following two complete rotations of the circuit, have a student demonstrate how to perform a forward roll out of the stork stand, straddle stand, and knee scale. Identify critical elements and return students to the circuit for practice.

5-4

The following tasks should be accomplished in this lesson:

Assess

Supports

Wheelbarrow walk

Springing and Landing

Jump from varied heights in star and tuck shapes
Frog jump uphill (feet apart)
Frog jump uphill (feet together)

Review

Balances

Headstand
Wall walk to handstand

Rotations

Forward roll from three different positions
Backward roll on mat to stand

New Skills

Balances

Kick up to one-leg handstand

Rotations

Forward roll to three different positions

Equipment

Mats
Open area clear of obstacles
Benches or raised platforms
Wall
Warm-up task cards
Equipment for warm-up
Chalk or tape

WARM-UP ACTIVITIES (5-6 MINUTES)

Use warm-up task cards.

REVIEW (DURING ROTATIONS CIRCUIT)

Review of balances and rotations has been included in the same circuit used to introduce new rotations (see the following introduction circuit).

ASSESS (5-6 MINUTES)

Supports

Assess the wheelbarrow walk as the whole class practices.

Springing and Landing

Assess jump from varied heights in star and tuck shapes, frog jump uphill (feet apart), and frog jump uphill (feet together) by creating a circuit of five or six stations (you may need two or three stations for the landing tasks). Explain what students will perform at each station, and assess children as they rotate (either from station to station freely or by your directions).

NEW SKILLS (18-20 MINUTES)

1. Create a circuit with the following stations: *Station 1.* Forward roll to three different positions. *Station 2.* Wall walk to handstand. *Station 3.* Backward roll on mat to stand. *Station 4.* Back rocker (see unit 1 for details). *Station 5.* Stork stand to forward roll. *Station 6.* Straddle stand to forward roll. *Station 7.* Knee scale to forward roll. *Station 8.* Headstand in pairs (one student performing and one holding the performer's legs). *Station 9.* Forward roll on mat to stand. Seat the class on the side of the circuit, and describe and demonstrate what they will do at each station. Then have a student demonstrate the whole circuit without stopping. Designate class members (three or four per station) and give them 30 to 40 seconds at each station before they move to the next station. Once all students have been through the circuit, change the following stations: At station 9 have students perform a forward roll to lying on back; at station 3 have students perform a forward roll to knee scale.

2. Add a new station where students can perform the forward roll to stork stand. At each of these stations, introduce the skill and identify the critical elements. These skills should be easy for the students to acquire.

Balances

Introduce this skill by demonstrating it, identifying the critical elements, then demonstrating again with students observing the critical elements. Use the following two rules to guide the instruction.

1. Progress from a small kick upward to increasingly larger kicks.

2. Don't have students attempt to kick past the handstand position (or they will fall over). Ensure that students are well distanced from each other to avoid accidents.

5-5

The following tasks should be accomplished in this lesson:

Assess

Rotations

Backward roll on mat to stand

Balances

Headstand

Review

Balances

Wall walk to handstand
Kick up to one-leg handstand

Rotations

Forward roll from three different positions
Forward roll to three different positions

New Skills

Rotations

Backward roll down incline to straddle stand
Minicartwheel over a bench
Cartwheel along a curved line

Equipment

Mats
Open area clear of obstacles
Benches or raised platforms
Inclines
Wall
Chalk or tape
Warm-up task cards
Equipment for warm-up

WARM-UP ACTIVITIES (5 MINUTES)

Use warm-up task cards.

REVIEW AND ASSESS (16 MINUTES)

1. Create the following circuit: *Station 1.* Headstand in pairs (one student performs and the other assists). *Station 2.* Wall walk to handstand. *Station 3.* Kick up to one-leg handstand. Explain what the students will perform at each station (use a demonstrator). Divide the class into three groups and have them rotate through the stations at regular intervals. As the students perform the skills, assess their performance of the headstand.

2. Create a second circuit with the following stations: *Station 1.* Backward roll on mat to stand. *Station 2.* Forward roll to knee scale. *Station 3.* Stork stand to forward roll.

Station 4. Straddle stand to forward roll. *Station 5.* Knee scale to forward roll. *Station 6.* Headstand in pairs (one student performs and one holds the performer's legs). *Station 7.* Forward roll to lying on back. *Station 8.* Forward roll to stork stand. Seat the class on the side of the circuit, and describe and demonstrate what they will do at each station. Then have a student demonstrate the whole circuit without stopping. Designate class members (three or four per station) and give them 30 to 40 seconds at each station before moving to the next station. Assess the backward roll on mat to stand.

NEW SKILLS (8 MINUTES)

Create the following circuit: *Station 1.* Backward roll down incline to straddle stand (use two or more inclines if possible). *Station 2.* Minicartwheel over a bench. *Station 3.* Cartwheel along a curved line (draw a curved chalk line and have as many lines as you have students in a group, if space permits). Make sure students are well spaced to avoid accidents. Explain what the students will perform at each station (use a demonstrator). Identify critical elements, and have a student demonstrate again, with students observing the critical elements. Divide the class into three groups and have them rotate through the stations at regular intervals.

5-6

The following tasks should be accomplished in this lesson:

Assess

Rotations
Forward roll to three different positions

Balances
Wall walk to handstand
Kick up to one-leg handstand

Review

Balances
Headstand

Rotations
Forward roll from three different positions
Backward roll down incline to straddle stand
Minicartwheel over a bench
Cartwheel along a curved line
Backward roll on mat to stand

Equipment
Mats
Open area clear of obstacles
Benches or raised platforms
Inclines
Wall
Chalk or tape
Warm-up task cards
Equipment for warm-up

WARM-UP ACTIVITIES (5 MINUTES)

Use warm-up task cards.

REVIEW AND ASSESS (20 MINUTES)

1. Create the balance circuit used in lesson 5: *Station 1.* Headstand in pairs (one student performs and the other assists). *Station 2.* Wall walk to handstand. *Station 3.* Kick up to one-leg handstand. Explain what students will perform at each station (use a demonstrator). Divide the class into three groups and have them rotate through the stations at regular intervals. As the students perform the skills, assess their performance of the wall walk to handstand and kick up to one-leg handstand.

2. Create a second circuit (same as in lesson 5) with the following stations: *Station 1.* Forward roll on mat to stand. *Station 2.* Backward roll on mat to stand. *Station 3.* Forward roll to knee scale. *Station 4.* Stork stand to forward roll. *Station 5.* Straddle stand to forward roll. *Station 6.* Knee scale to forward roll. *Station 7.* Headstand in pairs (one student performing and one holding the performer's legs). *Station 8.* Forward roll to lying on back. *Station 9.* Forward roll to stork stand. Seat the class on the side of the circuit, and describe and demonstrate what they will do at each station. Then have a student demonstrate the whole circuit without stopping. Designate class members (three or four per station) and give them 30 to 40 seconds at each station before they move to the next station. Assess the forward roll to stork stand, knee scale, and lying on back.

3. Create a third circuit: *Station 1.* Backward roll down incline to straddle stand (use two or more inclines if possible). *Station 2.* Minicartwheel over a bench. *Station 3.* Cartwheel along a curved line (draw a curved chalk line and have as many lines as you have students in a group, if space permits). Make sure students are well spaced to avoid accidents. Explain what students will perform at each station (use a demonstrator). Identify critical elements, and have a student demonstrate again, with students observing the critical elements. Divide the class into three groups, and have them rotate through the stations at regular intervals.

5-7

The following tasks should be accomplished in this lesson:

Assess

Rotations

Forward roll to three different positions
Backward roll down incline to straddle stand
Minicartwheel over a bench
Cartwheel along a curved line

Review

Rotations

Forward roll from three different positions
Backward roll on mat to stand

Equipment

Mats
Open area clear of obstacles
Benches or raised platforms
Inclines
Chalk or tape
Warm-up task cards
Equipment for warm-up

WARM-UP ACTIVITIES (5 MINUTES)

Use warm-up task cards.

REVIEW AND ASSESS (22 MINUTES)

1. Create a circuit (same as in lessons 5 and 6) with the following stations: *Station 1.* Forward roll on mat to stand. *Station 2.* Backward roll on mat to stand. *Station 3.* Forward roll to knee scale. *Station 4.* Stork stand to forward roll. *Station 5.* Straddle stand to forward roll. *Station 6.* Knee scale to forward roll. *Station 7.* Headstand in pairs (one student performs and one holds the performer's legs). *Station 8.* Forward roll to lying on back. *Station 9.* Forward roll to stork stand. Seat the class on the side of the circuit, and describe and demonstrate what they will do at each station. Designate class members (three or four per station), and give them 30 to 40 seconds at each station before they move to the next station. As-

sess the forward roll to stork stand, knee scale, and lying on back.

2. Create a second circuit: *Station 1.* Backward roll down incline to straddle stand (use two or more inclines if possible). *Station 2.* Minicartwheel over a bench. *Station 3.* Cartwheel along a curved line (draw a curved chalk line and have as many lines as you have students in a group, if space permits). Make sure they are well spaced to avoid accidents. Explain what students will perform at each station (use a demonstrator). Divide the class into three groups, and have them rotate through the stations at regular intervals. Assess each skill as the students rotate through the stations.

6-1

The following tasks should be accomplished in this lesson:

Review and Assess

Supports

Wheelbarrow walk

Rotations

Forward roll from three different positions
Backward roll down incline to stand
Backward roll down incline to straddle stand

Springing and Landing

Frog jump uphill (feet together)
Frog jump uphill (feet apart)

Equipment

Mats
Open area clear of obstacles
Benches or raised platforms (one or two feet high and sturdy enough for children to jump from)
Inclines to roll down, such as a triangular, wedge-shaped foam mat or two mats on top of a springboard
Warm-up task cards from appendix A
Equipment for warm-up

WARM-UP ACTIVITIES (8 MINUTES)

Before the lesson copy the warm-up task cards found in appendix A and adhere them to a cardboard backing (laminating these will make the task cards more durable).

1. Place the task cards in a widely spaced circle where you are conducting the lesson.

2. Take the class from task card to task card, explaining what to do at each station. Choose one student to demonstrate each station. Each task card should have its own station with enough equipment (e.g., ropes) for at least four students to practice. Students can rotate through the circuit in one of two ways. They could rotate from station to station as the teacher directs (e.g., 30 seconds to practice and 5 seconds to transition), or they can rotate when they complete each task. Focus on the correct performance, because you will use the same circuit for all lessons in this unit.

REVIEW AND ASSESS (20 MINUTES)

Springing and Landing

Review frog jump uphill (feet together) and frog jump uphill (feet apart) by having a student demonstrate each. Identify critical elements; then let students practice in self space. Be careful to allocate enough room to avoid students kicking each other accidentally, and have students follow the rule to stop moving if they get too close to another person.

Supports

Review front supports (see units 1 and 2 for details). Allow students two or three practice opportunities. Review the seal walk (see unit 3 for details). Allow students one or two practice opportunities. Introduce the wheelbarrow walk by stating, "The wheelbarrow walk is a seal walk without the need to drag your legs. Instead your partner holds your legs." Demonstrate the wheelbarrow walk (use two students). Identify critical elements, and point out that the person who is holding the legs of the performer must be careful to go very slowly. Have the class watch again and divide the class into pairs with similar weights. Specify the direction you want the students to wheelbarrow walk. Before starting practice offer an award (special activity, recognition, etc.) to any pair of students who can perform the wheelbarrow walk without either partner falling. The award provides additional motivation for students who might otherwise be careless. Do not encourage students to race each other as this can result in falls.

Rotations

Create a circuit of six stations (per 20 students): *Station 1.* Forward roll on mat to stand. *Station 2.* Backward roll down incline to stand. *Station 3.* Backward roll down incline to straddle stand. *Station 4.* Stork stand held for two seconds to forward roll on mat to stand. *Station 5.* Straddle stand held for two seconds to forward roll on mat to stand. *Station 6.* Knee scale held for two seconds to forward roll on mat to stand. Seat the class on the side of the circuit, and describe and demonstrate what they will do at each station. Then have a student demonstrate the whole circuit without stopping. Designate class members (three or four per station) and give them 30 to 40 seconds at each station before they move to the next station. Students should perform all skills on mats.

6-2

The following tasks should be accomplished in this lesson:

New Skills

Supports

Partner supports

Balances

Headstand
Wall walk to handstand
Kick up to one-leg handstand

Equipment

Mats
Open area clear of obstacles
Wall for students to walk up with their feet
Warm-up task cards
Equipment for warm-up
Chalk or tape

WARM-UP ACTIVITIES (5-6 MINUTES)

Review warm-up task cards by explaining and demonstrating what to do at each station. Use the same station locations that you used in lesson 1.

NEW SKILLS (22 MINUTES)

Supports

Introduce partner supports using the task cards in appendix A. Teach each partner support individually. Teach in the numerical order of the cards, and use the critical elements outlined on each card.

Hint 1: Mention to the class that there are two general critical elements. First, when you support yourself on another person, you may put your hands or legs only on their shoulders, hips, or ankles, which are the strongest parts of our bodies for these activities. Second, take care not to accidentally kick your partner when you get on and off. Divide the class into pairs, and provide at least three or four practice opportunities per card. Demonstrate each support (use two students).

Hint 2: Before starting practice offer an award (special activity, recognition, etc.) to any pair of students who can perform the tasks without either partner falling. The award provides additional motivation for students who might otherwise be careless.

Balances

1. Introduce the headstand, using four progressions (see progressions in chapter 2). First, demonstrate how to place the head and hands in a triangle. Next, have students practice lifting one leg at a time into the air (one leg always remains on the floor). When students can do this, introduce the bent-leg headstand by asking students to gradually lift both feet off the floor while maintaining balance. Finally, with students in pairs have one student perform a one-leg headstand, with the other student holding that leg at the calf. Then have the performing student lift the other leg up to join the extended leg. With each progression, have a student demonstrate it. Identify the critical elements or steps, and demonstrate again, with students looking for the critical elements. Allow at least five or six minutes of practice time for this skill and for short rests (30 seconds) between attempts. While students rest between attempts, have them watch their partners and provide feedback on the placement of the head and hands. The goal is for no student to roll or fall forward or onto his back. *Therefore, always use the assisting students when the headstand is performed.*

2. Introduce the wall walk to handstand. Starting one foot above the floor, draw four lines on the wall, approximately one foot higher than the other (use chalk or tape). Students should systematically walk up the wall to each of the four lines. Be careful that students do not move too close to the wall. Students may not feel comfortable going above the second or third line on the first few attempts. Focus on the competency of walking up and walking down the wall rather than how high they can walk.

3. Introduce the kick up to one-leg handstand by demonstrating it. Identify the critical ele-

ments; then demonstrate again with students observing the critical elements. Use the following two rules to guide the instruction: (1) progress from a small kick upward to increasingly larger kicks and (2) don't have students attempt to kick past the handstand position (or they will fall over). Ensure that students are well distanced from each other to avoid accidents.

6-3

The following tasks should be accomplished in this lesson:

Review

Supports
Partner supports

Balances
Headstand
Wall walk to handstand
Kick up to one-leg handstand

New Skills

Rotations
Cartwheel along a curved line
Cartwheel down an incline

Springing and Landing
Straddle over obstacle

Equipment
Mats
Open area clear of obstacles
Inclines
Wall
Warm-up task cards
Equipment for warm-up
Chalk or tape

WARM-UP ACTIVITIES (5 MINUTES)

Use the warm-up task cards. By now the students should know the circuit. (Always use the same location for the stations and activities that you used in previous lessons.)

REVIEW (8 MINUTES)

Supports
Review the partner supports by placing the cards in a circuit and asking two students to demonstrate each task. Review critical elements. Divide the class into pairs of students.

Balances
Create a circuit with three stations: *Station 1.* Headstand. *Station 2.* Wall walk to handstand. *Station 3.* Kick up to one-leg handstand. Review each skill (demonstrate and state critical elements). Divide the class into three groups. Allow groups one or two minutes practice at each station before they rotate.

NEW SKILLS (18 MINUTES)

Rotations

1. Teach the cartwheel along a curved line by drawing several lines on the floor. The lines should be six or seven feet long, slightly curved, and well spaced to avoid accidental kicking. Have a student demonstrate the cartwheel, and identify the critical elements. Have the student demonstrate again, with the class looking to see if the critical elements have been demonstrated. Assign students to each line and begin practice.

2. Introduce the cartwheel down an incline. Demonstrate and state the critical elements; then return the class to practice on the lines. During practice time send one or two groups over to the inclines (one to three inclines), and have them practice a cartwheel down the incline. Rotate students through the inclines and back to the lines for the remainder of the lesson.

Springing and Landing

Place the students in pairs. One student crouches with hands on the mat and the other stands two or three feet away from crouched partner. The standing partner walks forward and places her hands on the crouched student's shoulders. The standing student jumps off the back feet with hands remaining in contact with shoulders, straddles over crouched student, lifting their hands off while passing over the crouched student, and lands in a T-stand.

6-4

The following tasks should be accomplished in this lesson:

Review

Supports

Partner supports

Balances

Headstand
Wall walk to handstand
Kick up to one-leg handstand

Rotations

Cartwheel along a curved line
Cartwheel down an incline

Springing and Landing

Straddle over obstacle

New Skills

Rotations

Wheelbarrow forward roll
Backward roll on mat to straddle stand
Cartwheel on mat to stand

Equipment

Mats
Open area clear of obstacles
Inclines
Wall
Warm-up task cards
Equipment for warm-up
Chalk or tape

WARM-UP ACTIVITIES (5 MINUTES)

Use warm-up task cards.

REVIEW (10 MINUTES)

Supports

Review the partner supports by placing the cards in a circuit and asking two students to demonstrate each task (same organization as lesson 3). Review critical elements during each demonstration. Divide the class into pairs of students who have similar weights and review the rules established in lesson 2 (see hint 2).

Springing and Landing

Divide the class into pairs to review the straddle over obstacle. Review the roles of the performer and the partner, who is crouching, and allow 5 to 10 repetitions.

Balances

Review the headstand, wall walk to handstand, and kick up to one-leg handstand either individually or as part of a circuit.

Rotations

Create the circuit of six to nine stations: *Station 1.* Headstand. *Station 2.* Wall walk to handstand. *Station 3.* Kick up to one-leg handstand. *Station 4.* Cartwheel along a curved line. *Station 5.* Cartwheel down an incline. *Stations 6 through 9.* More cartwheel down an incline or cartwheel along a curved line stations. Review each skill (demonstrate and state critical elements). Divide the class into groups equal to the number of stations. Allow groups enough time to practice each skill three or four times before rotating.

NEW SKILLS (12 MINUTES)

Rotations

1. Add a station for the cartwheel on mat to stand to the previous circuit.

2. Divide the class into pairs with similar weights. Review and practice the wheelbarrow walk. Demonstrate the wheelbarrow forward roll, emphasizing the critical elements. Mention that the partner must help the performer by gently pushing the performer's legs forward as he begins the roll. Students must be able to perform the wheelbarrow walk before performing the wheelbarrow forward roll. Emphasize that the performer must keep his or her arms straight until the legs are lifted above the performer's head. Then lean forward as the head is tucked to begin the roll.

3. Keep the class in the same grouping you used with the wheelbarrow forward roll. Review and practice the backward roll on mat to stand. Demonstrate the backward roll on mat to straddle stand, emphasizing the critical elements. Students must be able to perform the backward roll on mat to stand and the backward roll down incline to straddle stand before performing the backward roll on mat to straddle stand.

6-5

The following tasks should be accomplished in this lesson:

Assess

Supports
Partner supports

Springing and Landing
Straddle over obstacle

Review

Balances
Headstand
Wall walk to handstand
Kick up to one-leg handstand

Rotations
Wheelbarrow forward roll
Backward roll on mat to straddle stand
Cartwheel along a curved line
Cartwheel down an incline

Equipment
Mats
Open area clear of obstacles
Inclines
Wall
Warm-up task cards
Equipment for warm-up
Chalk or tape

WARM-UP ACTIVITIES (5 MINUTES)

Use warm-up task cards.

ASSESS (8 MINUTES)

Supports
Assess the partner supports as students perform them in a circuit.

Springing and Landing
To assess the straddle over obstacle, divide the class into pairs. Review the roles of the performer and the partner, who is crouching. Assess the class during the practice time.

REVIEW (12 MINUTES)

Balances
Create a circuit of seven stations: *Station 1.* Headstand. *Station 2.* Wall walk to handstand. *Station 3.* Kick up to one-leg handstand. *Station 4.* Cartwheel along a curved line. *Station 5.* Cartwheel down an incline. *Station 6.* Backward roll on mat to straddle stand. *Station 7.* Wheelbarrow forward roll. Allow groups enough time to practice each skill three or four times before they rotate.

6-6

The following tasks should be accomplished in this lesson:

Assess

Balances

Headstand
Wall walk to handstand
Kick up to one-leg handstand

Review

Rotations

Wheelbarrow forward roll
Backward roll on mat to straddle stand
Cartwheel along a curved line
Cartwheel down an incline

Equipment

Mats
Open area clear of obstacles
Inclines
Wall
Warm-up task cards
Equipment for warm-up
Chalk or tape

WARM-UP ACTIVITIES (5 MINUTES)

Use warm-up task cards.

REVIEW AND ASSESS (22 MINUTES)

Create a circuit of seven stations: *Station 1.* Headstand. *Station 2.* Wall walk to handstand. *Station 3.* Kick up to one-leg handstand. *Station 4.* Cartwheel along a curved line. *Station 5.* Cartwheel down an incline. *Station 6.* Backward roll on mat to straddle stand. *Station 7.* Wheelbarrow forward roll. Allow groups enough time to practice each skill three or four times before they rotate. Assess the headstand, wall walk to handstand, and kick up to one-leg handstand as students rotate through the stations.

6-7

The following tasks should be accomplished in this lesson:

Assess

Rotations

Wheelbarrow forward roll
Backward roll on mat to straddle stand
Cartwheel along a curved line
Cartwheel down an incline

Review

Balances

Headstand
Wall walk to handstand
Kick up to one-leg handstand

Equipment

Mats
Open area clear of obstacles
Inclines
Wall
Warm-up task cards
Equipment for warm-up
Chalk or tape

WARM-UP ACTIVITIES (5 MINUTES)

Use warm-up task cards.

REVIEW AND ASSESS (20-25 MINUTES)

Create a circuit of seven stations: *Station 1.* Headstand. *Station 2.* Wall walk to handstand. *Station 3.* Kick up to one-leg handstand. *Station 4.* Cartwheel along a curved line. *Station 5.* Cartwheel down an incline. *Station 6.* Backward roll on mat to straddle stand. *Station 7.* Wheelbarrow forward roll. Allow groups enough time to practice each skill three or four times before they rotate. Assess the wheelbarrow forward roll, backward roll on mat to straddle stand, cartwheel along a curved line, and cartwheel down an incline. Students rotate through the stations.

Task Cards

GREAT STRETCH

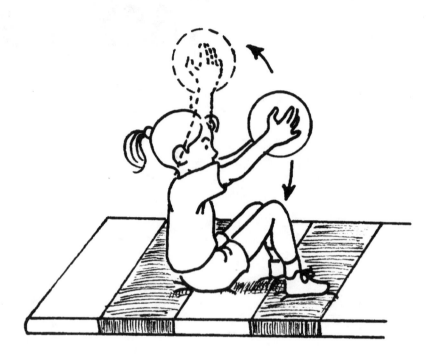

1. Find a ball and a mat to sit on.

2. Sit with your legs bent and your feet on the floor.

3. Take the ball and, while keeping your arms straight, see how far you can lift the ball behind your head. Then lower it to touch your knees. Try this eight times slowly.

4. Put the ball back, then move to the next station.

REACH FOR THE STARS STRETCH

1. Find somewhere to stand.

2. Hook your fingers together and reach upward toward the ceiling.

3. Hold this until you count to 10, then reach upward and count to 10 again.

4. Move to the next station.

SIT-UPS

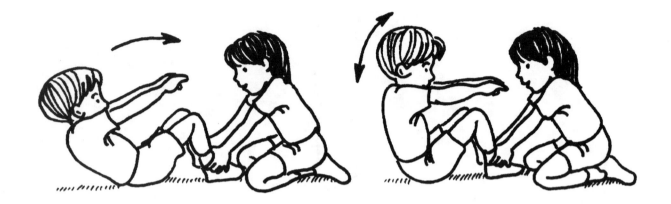

1. Find a mat to sit on.

2. Bend your legs while someone is holding your feet.

3. Remember not to arch your back.

4. Perform 15 continuous sit-ups, 3 times (45 total) or perform 10 continuous sit-ups, 4 times (40 total).

5. Move to the next station.

SKIP TO MY LOU

1. Find a skipping rope and a safe place to skip without hitting other students.

2. Perform 50 continuous skips with your rope or perform 60 continuous skips with your rope.

3. Move to the next station.

UP-DOWN ANKLE STRETCH

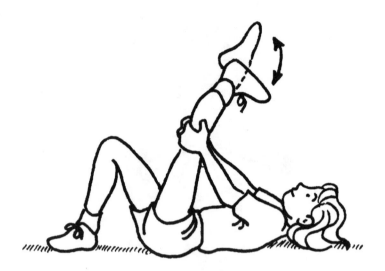

1. Find a mat and lie on your back.

2. Bend one leg and place your foot on the mat.

3. Lift your other leg upward toward your chest, keeping it straight.

4. Hold this for a count of 10, then perform this with your other leg.

5. Move to the next station.

SUPER LEG STRETCHING

1. Find somewhere to stand.

2. Reach over and place your hands on the floor. One or both legs may bend.

3. Next straighten one leg and stretch it gently backward. Keep the other leg bent.

4. Hold this until you count to 10, then repeat this with the other leg.

5. Move to the next station.

CIRCLE STRETCH

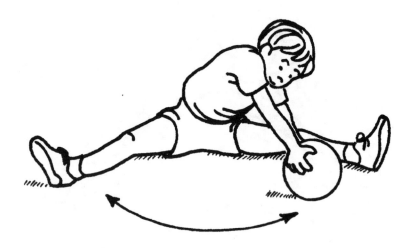

1. Find a ball and a mat to sit on.

2. Sit with your legs straight and apart.

3. Take the ball and see if you can circle around (or over) your feet without bending your legs.

4. Circle twice each way slowly.

5. Put the ball back, then move to the next station.

COUNTERBALANCE-1

1. Find a partner.

2. Stand side-by-side with one foot touching your partner.

3. Hold hands and lean sideways picking up your outside foot.

4. Adjust your position until you can hold the pose without moving or falling.

5. Freeze in this balance for 5 seconds.

COUNTERBALANCE-2

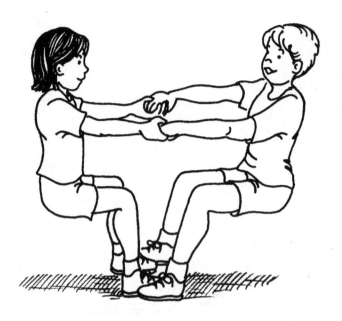

1. Find a partner.

2. Face your partner and hold each other's hands.

3. Bend your knees slowly like you are sitting down into a chair.

4. Keep holding hands and adjust your position until you can hold the pose.

5. Hold for 5 seconds.

COUNTERBALANCE-3

1. Find a partner.

2. Stand back-to-back with your partner.

3. Slowly push against each other and bend your knees.

4. Hold the pose without moving or falling for 5 seconds.

COUNTERBALANCE-4

1. Find a partner.

2. Face each other and hold hands.

3. Each person steps back with one foot, keeping the arms straight, then the back foot is moved forward to join the front foot.

4. Freeze in this position for 5 seconds.

COUNTERBALANCE-5

1. Find a partner.

2. Put your feet together and lie on your back with your knees bent, toes touching.

3. Slowly straighten your legs and lift up on your elbows.

4. Adjust your position until you can hold the pose without moving or falling for 5 seconds.

COUNTERBALANCE-6

1. Find a partner and lie on your back with knees and feet together, your feet touching your partner's.

2. Straighten your legs slowly and lift up on your elbows.

3. Bend your knees.

4. Adjust your pose until you can balance without moving or falling for 5 seconds.

COUNTERBALANCE-7

1. Find a partner.

2. Put your back to your partner's back with your heels touching.

3. Step forward with one foot and simultaneously straighten your arms. Then step backward with the front foot to rejoin the other.

4. Adjust your position until you can hold the pose without moving or falling for 5 seconds.

PARTNER SUPPORT-1

1. Find a partner and decide who is going in front (Partner #1) and who is going behind (Partner #2).

2. Partner #1: Get into a front support position with your feet slightly apart.

3. Partner #2: Place one hand at a time on the ankles of your partner.

4. Partner #1 and Partner #2: Hold this balance for at least 10 seconds.

5. Partner #2: Lift one hand at a time off the ankles of your partner.

6. Partner #1 and Partner #2: Stand up, swap positions, and try it again.

PARTNER SUPPORT-2

1. Find a partner and decide who is going in front (Partner #1) and who is going behind (Partner #2).

2. Partner #2: Kneel with your arms bent and your head tucked.

3. Partner #1: Get into a front support position. Put your feet on either side of your partner's hands.

4. Partner #1: Place one foot at a time on the shoulders of your partner. Take care not to hit your partner's head!

5. Partner #2: Straighten your arms and hold the kneeling position.

6. Partner #1 and Partner #2: Hold this balance for at least 10 seconds.

7. Partner #1: Lift one foot at a time off the shoulders of your partner.

8. Partner #1 and Partner #2: Stand up, swap positions, and try it again.

PARTNER SUPPORT-3

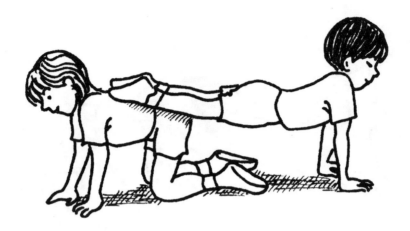

1. Find a partner and decide who is going in front (Partner #1) and who is going behind (Partner #2).

2. Partner #1: Kneel with your hips over your knees.

3. Partner #2: Get into a front support position beside your partner so that your feet are beside your partner's hips.

4. Partner #2: Slowly place one foot at a time on your partner's hips. Don't put your feet on your partner's back!

5. Partner #1 and Partner #2: Hold this balance for at least 10 seconds.

6. Partner #2: Lift one foot at a time off your partner's hips.

7. Partner #1 and Partner #2: Stand up, swap positions, and try it again.

PARTNER SUPPORT-4

1. Find a partner and decide who is going on top (Partner #1) and who is going on bottom (Partner #2).

2. Partner #2: Lie on the ground with your back flat against the floor, your knees bent, and feet flat.

3. Partner #1: Get into a front support position with your feet on either side of your partner's head.

4. Partner #2: Bend your arms and grasp each ankle of your partner, then straighten your arms.

5. Partner #1 and Partner #2: Hold this balance for 5 to 10 seconds.

6. Partner #2: Bend your arms and let your partner step off.

7. Partner #1 and Partner #2: Stand up, swap positions, and try it again.

PARTNER SUPPORT-5

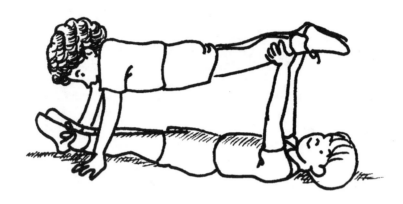

1. Find a partner and decide who is going on top (Partner #1) and who is going on bottom (Partner #2).

2. Partner #2: Lie on your back.

3. Partner #1: Get in a front support position with your hands on either side of the feet of your partner and your feet on either side of your partner's shoulders.

4. Partner #2: Grasp your partner's ankle, then straighten your arms one at a time. Lift your partner up over you.

5. Partner #1 and Partner #2: Hold this balance for at least 10 seconds.

6. Partner #2: Bend your arms and let go of your partner's ankles.

7. Partner #1 and Partner #2: Stand up, swap positions, and try it again.

PARTNER SUPPORT-6

1. Find a partner and decide who is going on top (Partner #1) and who is going on bottom (Partner #2).

2. Partner #2: Kneel with your hips directly over your knees.

3. Partner #1: Place your hands on your partner's shoulders. Do not put your hands on your partner's back. Slowly lift one leg at a time onto the hips of your partner.

4. Partner #1 and Partner #2: Hold this balance for at least 5 seconds.

5. Partner #1: Remove one leg at a time off your partner and transfer your weight onto your feet.

6. Partner #1 and Partner #2: Stand up, swap positions, and try it again.

PARTNER SUPPORT-7

1. Find a partner and decide who is going on top (Partner #1) and who is going on bottom (Partner #2).

2. Partner #2: Kneel with your hips directly over your knees.

3. Partner #1: Stand beside your partner and place one hand on each hip. Do not place your hands on your partner's back. Slowly transfer your weight to the person below and lift one leg then the other onto your partner's shoulders.

4. Partner #1 and Partner #2: Hold this balance for at least 5 seconds.

5. Partner #1: Remove one leg at a time off your partner and transfer weight onto your feet.

6. Partner #1 and Partner #2: Stand up, swap positions, and try it again.

Skills Checklist

BALANCES AND SUPPORTS

1. Standing tall
- ❏ Body straight and stretched
- ❏ Shoulders down and neck long
- ❏ Arms by sides
- ❏ Look forward

2. T-stand
- ❏ Body straight and stretched
- ❏ Shoulders down and neck long
- ❏ Lift arms to sides horizontally
- ❏ Look forward

3. Landing shape
- ❏ Bend knees slightly
- ❏ Hold upper body straight and lean forward slightly
- ❏ Lift arms forward horizontally
- ❏ Look forward

4. Stork stand
- ❏ Look forward
- ❏ Body straight and stretched
- ❏ One foot inside the other knee
- ❏ Hands on hips
- ❏ Hold for three seconds

5. Pike
- ❏ Look forward
- ❏ Back straight and stretched
- ❏ Shoulders down and neck long
- ❏ Arms by sides
- ❏ Legs straight and toes pointed

6. Tuck sit
- ❏ Knees bent and near chest
- ❏ Balanced on buttocks
- ❏ Toes resting on floor
- ❏ Hold for three seconds

7. Lying face down
- ❏ Face down on mat
- ❏ Body stretched and arms overhead
- ❏ Legs straight and toes pointed
- ❏ Hold for three seconds

8. Lying face up
- ❏ Face up on mat
- ❏ Body stretched and arms overhead
- ❏ Legs straight and toes pointed
- ❏ Hold for three seconds

9. Bent-knee stand
- ❏ Body straight and stretched
- ❏ Bend one leg at the knee and raise to hip level
- ❏ Lift arms to sides horizontally
- ❏ Hold for three seconds

10. Two-knee balance
- ❏ Balance on two knees
- ❏ Upper body straight and stretched
- ❏ Lift arms to sides horizontally
- ❏ Hold for three seconds

11. Toe stand
- ❏ Body straight
- ❏ Stand on toes
- ❏ Lift arms to sides horizontally
- ❏ Hold for three seconds

12. One-foot toe stand
- ❏ Body straight
- ❏ Stand on one foot on toes
- ❏ Lift arms to sides horizontally
- ❏ Hold for three seconds

13. Straddle sit
- ❏ Legs straddled
- ❏ Upper body stretched upward at 90 degrees to the legs
- ❏ Arms straight and stretched overhead, shoulder-width apart

14. Knee scale

- [ ] Kneel on one leg
- [ ] Other leg straight, lift it backward and upward
- [ ] Hands on floor
- [ ] Head up
- [ ] Look forward

15. Straddle stand

- [ ] Stand with legs straight and straddled (apart sideways)
- [ ] Bend upper body 90 degrees to lower body, facing forward
- [ ] Lift arms to sides horizontally
- [ ] Look forward

16. Shoulder-feet balance

- [ ] Only shoulders, feet, and arms touch the ground
- [ ] Use arms for support

17. Shoulder balance

- [ ] Arms press down onto the floor
- [ ] Hips over shoulders
- [ ] Body straight and toes pointing to the ceiling
- [ ] Look at toes

18. Counterbalances

The teacher chooses two counterbalances to assess.

- [ ] Hold first balance for five seconds
- [ ] Hold second balance for five seconds

19. Tripod balance

- [ ] Arms and head in triangular formation
- [ ] Lean backward slightly
- [ ] Weight mostly on the hands
- [ ] Knees bent and resting on elbows
- [ ] Feet off the ground
- [ ] Hold for two seconds

20. Headstand

- [ ] Arms and head in triangular formation
- [ ] Body stretched and straight
- [ ] Lean backward slightly
- [ ] Weight mostly on the hands
- [ ] Legs straight and together
- [ ] Hold for two seconds

21. Front support

- [ ] Arms straight
- [ ] Body straight and firm
- [ ] Legs straight and together
- [ ] Look forward

22. Kick up to one-leg handstand

- [ ] Stand with arms stretched forward horizontally
- [ ] Lunge forward
- [ ] Place hands on the floor shoulder-width apart
- [ ] Keep the back leg straight, kick upward
- [ ] Front leg pushes against the floor and straightens
- [ ] Finish with legs apart and straight

23. Wall walk to handstand

- [ ] Front support position with feet touching a wall
- [ ] Walk up the wall with each foot
- [ ] Walk in with each hand
- [ ] Finish in a "near" handstand position
- [ ] Hold for two seconds

24. Rear support

- [ ] Arms straight
- [ ] Body straight and firm
- [ ] Legs straight and together
- [ ] Look forward

25. Side support

- [ ] Balance on one arm (keep it straight)
- [ ] Body straight and facing sideways
- [ ] Legs together (both feet may touch the floor)

26. Game "Find the support"

- [ ] Start running and skipping
- [ ] Assume support position called out by teacher
- [ ] Perform at least five or six support positions

27. Game "Under and over"

- [ ] Divide class into pairs, numbered one and two
- [ ] Number ones assume a support position called out by the teacher
- [ ] Number twos crawl under or step over number ones
- [ ] Partners switch roles

28. Tuck to front support

- [ ] Start in a tuck
- [ ] Finish in front support with legs straight and together
- [ ] Arms straight

29. Front support to tuck
- ❏ Start in front support
- ❏ Jump forward to tuck
- ❏ Finish with feet close to hands

30. Front support to straddle stand
- ❏ Start in front support
- ❏ Jump forward to straddle stand
- ❏ Legs straight and apart
- ❏ Arms horizontal and stretched sideways
- ❏ Body bent 90 degrees at the hip

31. Straddle stand to front support
- ❏ From straddle stand lean forward onto the hands
- ❏ Jump back to front support
- ❏ Arms, legs, and back straight

32. Game "Front support tag"
- ❏ Define boundaries of game
- ❏ Choose one or two students to tag others
- ❏ Tagged students assume a front support position
- ❏ Free students crawl under tagged students to free them

33. Front support change to rear support
- ❏ Start in front support
- ❏ Keep body straight
- ❏ Turn over sideways to rear support

34. Wheelbarrow walk
- ❏ Start in front support with legs apart
- ❏ Walk forward on hands

35. Partner supports
- ❏ The teacher chooses two partner supports to assess.
- ❏ Hold balance for 5 to 10 seconds
- ❏ Take support on shoulders or hips

ROTATIONS

36. Back rocker
- ❏ Sit in a tucked position
- ❏ Back rounded
- ❏ Chin near chest
- ❏ Rock backward and forward

37. Back rocker to stand
- ❏ Rock back and forth
- ❏ Hands push off floor to standing
- ❏ Finish in T-stand

38. From stand to back rocker
- ❏ Start in standing tall with arms forward horizontally
- ❏ Use hands to support on floor when sitting
- ❏ Rock back and forth without stopping

39. Forward roll on mat to sit
- ❏ Start in standing position
- ❏ Tuck and place hands in front of shoulders
- ❏ Tuck the head toward the chest
- ❏ Roll forward in a straight line
- ❏ Finish in a sitting position
- ❏ Legs straight on the floor

40. Forward roll down incline to tuck
- ❏ Stand on top of the incline
- ❏ Tuck, placing hands in front of shoulders
- ❏ Tuck the head toward the chest
- ❏ Roll forward in a straight line
- ❏ Finish in a tuck position

41. Back rocker with hand touch
- ❏ Sit in a tucked position
- ❏ Back rounded
- ❏ Chin on chest
- ❏ Hands by ears, palms upward and backward
- ❏ Rock backward and forward
- ❏ Hands touch the ground behind head each time

42. Forward roll down incline to stand
- ❏ Stand on top of the incline
- ❏ Tuck, placing hands in front of shoulders
- ❏ Tuck the head toward the chest
- ❏ Roll forward in a straight line
- ❏ Finish in a T-stand

43. Forward roll on mat to stand
- ❏ Start in standing position
- ❏ Tuck, placing hands in front of shoulders
- ❏ Tuck the head toward the chest
- ❏ Roll forward in a straight line
- ❏ Finish in a T-stand

44. Backward roll down incline to tuck
- ❏ Sit on top of the incline
- ❏ Knees close to chest in a tucked position
- ❏ Hands palm upward by ears
- ❏ Roll backward with hands by ears
- ❏ Remain in tuck position
- ❏ Hands push against floor
- ❏ Finish in a tuck position

45. Forward roll from three different positions

- ☐ Start in either a straddle stand, knee scale, or stork stand
- ☐ Tuck quickly
- ☐ Place hands in front of shoulders (not necessary in knee scale)
- ☐ Tuck the head toward the chest
- ☐ Roll forward in a straight line
- ☐ Finish in a T-stand

46. Forward roll to three different positions

- ☐ Standing tall, arms forward horizontally
- ☐ Tuck quickly, placing hands close to feet
- ☐ Tuck the head toward the chest
- ☐ Roll forward in a straight line
- ☐ Finish in a knee scale, a stork stand, or lying face up

47. Backward roll down incline to stand

- ☐ Start in sitting or tucked position on top of the incline
- ☐ Hands palms upward by ears
- ☐ Roll backward with hands by ears
- ☐ Remain in tuck position
- ☐ Hands push against floor
- ☐ Finish in a T-stand

48. Backward roll on mat to stand

- ☐ Start in tucked or sitting position at the end of a mat
- ☐ Hands palm upward by ears
- ☐ Roll backward with hands by ears
- ☐ Remain in tuck position
- ☐ Hands push against floor
- ☐ Finish in a T-stand

49. Backward roll down incline to straddle stand

- ☐ Start in sitting or tucked position on top of the incline
- ☐ Hands palm upward by ears
- ☐ Roll backward with hands by ears
- ☐ Straighten legs and pull them apart
- ☐ Hands push against floor
- ☐ Finish in a straddle stand

50. Wheelbarrow forward roll

- ☐ Start in the wheelbarrow position
- ☐ Lean forward, bend arms, and tuck head
- ☐ Roll body forward in a tuck position
- ☐ Finish in a T-stand

51. Backward roll on mat to straddle stand

- ☐ Start in tucked position
- ☐ Hands palm upward by ears
- ☐ Roll backward with hands by ears
- ☐ Straighten legs and pull them apart
- ☐ Hands push against floor
- ☐ Finish in a straddle stand

52. Half log rolls

- ☐ Start on back or face down
- ☐ Body stretched
- ☐ Arms stretched overhead and together
- ☐ Legs straight and together
- ☐ Complete a 180-degree turn

53. Full log rolls

- ☐ Start on back or face down
- ☐ Body stretched
- ☐ Arms stretched overhead and together
- ☐ Legs straight and together
- ☐ Complete a 360-degree turn

54. Puppy dog roll

- ☐ Kneel with hands on the ground
- ☐ Sit back onto legs
- ☐ Roll 180°, contacting ground at shoulder, hip, and back
- ☐ Stay in the tucked position throughout

55. Partner log rolls

- ☐ Roll together in the same direction
- ☐ Complete a 360-degree rotation
- ☐ Legs remain straight and together
- ☐ Arms remain straight
- ☐ Hands remain joined

56. Sit and spin

- ☐ Sit on a mat, legs bent, hands on the floor
- ☐ Lift feet off the floor
- ☐ Use hands to spin the body
- ☐ Tightly tuck and wrap hands around knees
- ☐ Stay seated (no fall to back)

57. Jump, twist, and freeze

- ☐ Jump and twist 180 degrees
- ☐ Land in landing shape

58. Cartwheel weight transfer along bench

- ☐ Stand on one side of the bench
- ☐ Hands on the bench
- ☐ Step over the bench with the closer foot
- ☐ Follow with the other foot (a one-two action)
- ☐ Continue stepping over the bench from one side to the other

59. Cartwheel over an inclined rope

- ❏ Hands on the floor on both sides of the rope
- ❏ Feet on one side of the rope
- ❏ Step over the rope with the closer foot
- ❏ Follow with the other foot (a one-two action)
- ❏ Continue to step over the rope from one side to the other
- ❏ Legs should be nearly straight as they pass over the rope

60. Minicartwheel over a bench

- ❏ Stand on one side of the bench
- ❏ Step forward and place one hand, then the other, on the bench
- ❏ Kick the closer foot over the bench
- ❏ Follow with the other foot (a one-two action)
- ❏ Finish standing on the other side of the bench in a T-stand

61. Cartwheel along a curved line

- ❏ Stand inside the curved line
- ❏ Face and look along the line
- ❏ Lunge forward with the foot closer to the line
- ❏ Place one hand, then the other, on the line
- ❏ Kick the farther foot into the air and forward
- ❏ Follow with the other foot (a one-two action)
- ❏ Finish in a T-stand

62. Cartwheel down an incline

- ❏ Stand facing forward, looking down the incline
- ❏ Lunge forward with the closer foot
- ❏ Place one hand, then the other, on the incline
- ❏ Kick the farther foot into the air and forward
- ❏ Follow with the other foot
- ❏ Finish in a T-stand

63. Cartwheel on mat to stand

- ❏ Stand facing forward
- ❏ Lunge forward with the closer foot
- ❏ Place one hand, then the other, on the mat
- ❏ Kick the farther foot into the air and forward
- ❏ Follow with the other foot
- ❏ Finish in a T-stand

SPRINGING AND LANDING

64. Straight jump and land in self space

- ❏ Jump upward swinging arms overhead
- ❏ Jump into air with straight legs
- ❏ Land in landing shape without stepping

65. Straight jump and land into hoop

- ❏ Jump upward swinging arms overhead
- ❏ Jump into air with straight legs
- ❏ Land in landing shape in hoop without stepping

66. Star jump and land in self space

- ❏ Jump upward swinging arms overhead
- ❏ Jump into air with straight and straddled legs
- ❏ Land in landing shape without stepping

67. Jump over a hoop

- ❏ Stand on one side of a hoop
- ❏ Swing arms upward and forward
- ❏ Jump over the hoop without touching it
- ❏ Land in landing shape

68. Jump backward into a hoop

- ❏ Stand with back toward the hoop
- ❏ Small jump backward into the hoop
- ❏ Land in landing shape

69. Jump from a low height with straight shape

- ❏ Jump with straight body
- ❏ Bend legs slightly
- ❏ Land in the landing shape

70. Jump from a low height with tuck shape

- ❏ Jump with tucked body
- ❏ Land in the landing shape

71. Jump from varied heights in star and tuck shapes

- ❏ Jump with tucked or star body shapes
- ❏ Land in the landing shape

72. Two-foot bunny jumps

- ❏ Continuous short and small jumps

73. Kangaroo jumps

- ❏ Continuous long and large jumps

74. Mouse walk

- ❏ Continuous quick walk with hands and feet

75. Couple jumping
☐ Hold hands facing each other
☐ One partner stands, the other jumps
☐ Continuous short and small jumps in the same place

76. Jack-in-the-box
☐ Start in a tuck
☐ Large jump upward off the floor
☐ Land in the landing shape

77. Jump and clap
☐ Jump upward off the floor
☐ Clap hands in front
☐ Land in the landing shape

78. Bent-knee hop
☐ Bend one leg at the knee and raise to hip level
☐ Continuous hop on the other leg

79. Frog jump (feet together)
☐ Start in tuck position
☐ Hands reach forward
☐ Body leans forward
☐ Transfer weight from feet to hands
☐ Jump feet forward to tuck close to the hands

80. Frog jump (feet apart)
☐ Straddle stand with hands on the ground
☐ Hands reach forward
☐ Body leans forward
☐ Transfer weight from feet to hands
☐ Jump feet forward to straddle stand outside the hands

81. Crab walk
☐ Start face up, balancing on hands and feet
☐ Walk forward or backward

82. Seal walk
☐ Start in a front support position
☐ Keep legs straight and together
☐ Take steps with the hands and drag the feet

83. Lame monkey walk
☐ Start in lunge position
☐ Keep back leg straight throughout
☐ Walk by hopping on bent leg
☐ Push the floor behind with both hands

84. Frog jump uphill (feet apart)
☐ Start in straddle stand
☐ Reach forward with both hands
☐ Place hands on a bench or raised platform
☐ Spring off the back feet
☐ Keep hands in contact with the bench
☐ Place the feet on either side of the hands

85. Frog jump uphill (feet together)
☐ Start in tucked position, feet together
☐ Reach forward with both hands
☐ Place hands on a bench or raised platform
☐ Spring off the back feet
☐ Keep hands in contact with the bench
☐ Place the feet between the hands

86. Straddle over obstacle
☐ Start two or three feet away from crouched partner
☐ Walk forward
☐ Reach forward with both hands
☐ Place hands on the crouched student's shoulders
☐ Spring off the back feet
☐ Hands remain in contact with the shoulders
☐ Straddle over crouched student
☐ Lift arms
☐ Land in T-stand in front of partner

Achievement Certificate

This Certificate for
Excellence in Tumbling
is awarded to

_____
Name

for

_____
Description of routine/skills

_____
School/Grade

_____
Teacher

Recommended Resources and Materials

RECOMMENDED BOOKS AND MATERIALS

American Coaching Effectiveness Program. 1992. *Rookie coaches gymnastics guide*. Champaign, IL: Human Kinetics.

Noble, D.K. 1983. *Gymnastics for kids ages 3-7*. New York: Leisure Press.

Schembri, G. 1984. *Gym fun*. Melbourne: Australian Gymnastics Federation.

Werner, P.H. 1994. *Teaching children gymnastics: Becoming a master teacher*. Champaign, IL: Human Kinetics.

Werner, P.H. 1994. *Teaching children gymnastics video: Becoming a master teacher*. Champaign, IL: Human Kinetics.

TEACHING EFFECTIVENESS BIBLIOGRAPHY

Graham, G., S. Holt-Hale, and M. Parker. 1993. *Children moving: A reflective approach to teaching physical education*. 3rd ed. Mountainview, CA: Mayfield.

Pangrazi, R., and V. Dauer. 1995. *Dynamic physical education for elementary school children*. Boston: Allyn & Bacon.

Rink, J. 1985. *Teaching for learning in physical education*. St. Louis: Mosby.

Siedentop, D. 1991. *Developing teaching skills in physical education*. 3rd ed. Mountainview, CA: Mayfield.

Siedentop, D., J. Herkowitz, and J. Rink. 1983. *Physical education for elementary school children*. Englewood Cliffs, NJ: Prentice Hall.

ABOUT THE AUTHOR

A former gymnast, coach, and teacher, Phillip Ward has been involved in gymnastics for more than 25 years. As assistant professor in the Department of Health and Human Performance at the University of Nebraska-Lincoln, Ward's major scholarly interests include pedagogy, teacher education, and applied behavior analysis.

Before joining the university, Ward was coaching director of the Victorian Gymnastics Association, where he was responsible for coaching education and course development. He was also a gymnast, a coach to beginning and elite gymnasts, a teacher, and a teacher educator.

Ward earned his PhD in physical education from The Ohio State University in 1993. The author of numerous articles and six manuals on gymnastics and gymnastics instructions, he is a member of the American Association of Health, Physical Education, Recreation and Dance; the American Educational Research Association; and the National Association for Sport and Physical Education.

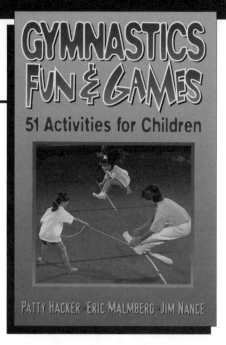

Caerleon
Library